Ancient Greece
about 1000-337 B.C.

Ancient Rome
about 753 B.C.-300 A.D.

The Empire of Mali
about 1230-1450 A.D.

Dates are sometimes noted as B.C., for BEFORE CHRIST and A.D. for ANNO DOMINI, which is Latin for YEAR OF OUR LORD, which mark the years since the birth of Jesus Christ. B.C.E. means BEFORE THE COMMON ERA and the year 1 in our modern calender marks the COMMON ERA. Since there are so many religions in the world, many historians now use B.C.E. instead of B.C., and C.E. instead of A.D, but this book uses the more traditional B.C. and A.D.

OUR WORLD
FAR & WIDE
VIRGINIA

| Columbus sails to the Americas 1492 | Ponce de Léon lands in Florida 1513 | Cartier claims land in Canada for France 1534 | Christopher Newport comes to Virginia 1607 | Thomas Jefferson writes Declaration of Independence 1776 | George Washington is elected President 1789 | Abraham Lincoln gives Gettysburg Address 1863 | Rosa Parks is arrested starting Civil Rights movement 1955 | Martin Luther King Jr. leads march on Washington 1963 | Thurgood Marshall joins Supreme Court 1967 |

FIVE PONDS PRESS

OUR WORLD
FAR & WIDE

BY JOY MASOFF

ADVISORY BOARD

Dr. Melissa Matusevich: Virginia Tech, Blacksburg, Virginia, and former supervisor of Social Studies and Library Media, Montgomery County, Virginia, Public Schools.

Dr. Donald Zeigler: Professor of Geography and Political Science, Old Dominion University, Virginia Beach, Virginia.

REVIEWERS

Five Ponds Press wishes to acknowledge the contributions and encouragement of many Virginia educators.
Special thanks to:
Lisa Arnold, Henrico County, Virginia
Bree Linton, Sandston, Virginia
Anita Parker, Virginia Beach, Virginia
Lara Samuels, Henrico County, Virginia
Leslie Swenson, Henrico, Virginia
Nancy Daniel Vest, Richmond, Virginia
and **Jason Deryck-Mahlke,** John Jay High School, Cross River, New York

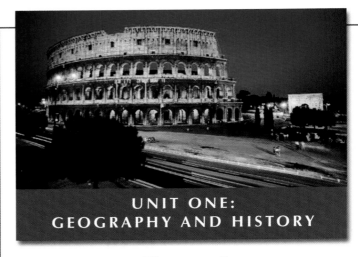

UNIT ONE:
GEOGRAPHY AND HISTORY

Copyright ©2010 by Joy Masoff. All rights reserved.
Published by Five Ponds Press, Weston, CT 06883.
Library of Congress Cataloging-in-Publication data available.
First printing July 2010.

ISBN 978-0-9824133-3-3
Printed in the USA
4 5 QGT 12

UNIT THREE: CIVICS

UNIT TWO: ECONOMICS

CHAPTER 1

WONDERFUL WORLD

See our amazing planet in new and different ways!

Our planet as seen from space. This view shows Africa, part of Asia, and Europe.

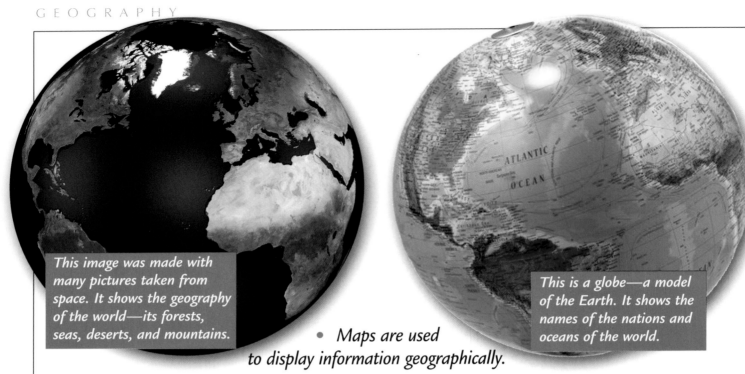

This image was made with many pictures taken from space. It shows the geography of the world—its forests, seas, deserts, and mountains.

ATLANTIC OCEAN

This is a globe—a model of the Earth. It shows the names of the nations and oceans of the world.

- Maps are used to display information geographically.
- The Equator and the Prime Meridian divide the globe into four hemispheres.
- The four hemispheres are Northern, Southern, Eastern, and Western.

Words To Know

- **Hemisphere**

  (HEM-iss-fear)
  Half of a sphere (globe) created by the Prime Meridian or the Equator.

- **Equator**
  (ee-KWAY-tur)
  An imaginary line around the middle of the Earth that divides the globe into the Northern and Southern Hemispheres.

- **Prime meridian**
  An imaginary line that (when extended completely around the Earth) divides the globe into the Eastern and Western Hemispheres.

GLOBES AND MAPS

Our Earth is a huge ball spinning in the sky. Globes show us what the Earth looks like from space. To see the whole Earth at once, mapmakers make pictures that look like a flattened ball. Then we can see the entire world at a glance.

Before we can learn all about the story of our world, we have to learn about our planet, Earth. Maps and globes are the best way to do that. Why? As we learn about how our world works, a lot depends on *where* events took place. Every mountain, ocean, and desert shaped the lives of the people who lived there. Maps and globes show us where these places are.

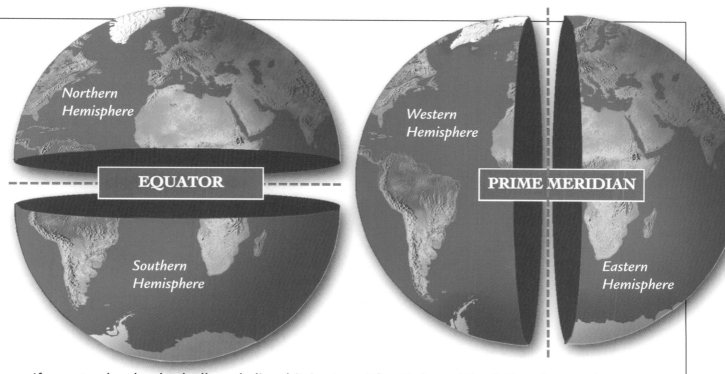

Northern Hemisphere

EQUATOR

Southern Hemisphere

Western Hemisphere

PRIME MERIDIAN

Eastern Hemisphere

If you took a basketball and sliced it in half, you would have a **hemisphere**. Sphere (*sfeer*) is another word for a round ball. Hemi means "half" in Latin, the language of ancient Rome.

The **Equator** is a make-believe line that divides the globe into the Northern and Southern Hemispheres. When it is winter in the Northern Hemisphere, it is summer in the Southern Hemisphere.

The **Prime Meridian** is another make-believe line. It connects the North and South Poles and passes through Greenwich, England, near London. If extended completely around the world, it divides the Earth into the Eastern and Western Hemispheres.

This "line" is the starting point for the world's time zones which makes it very important.

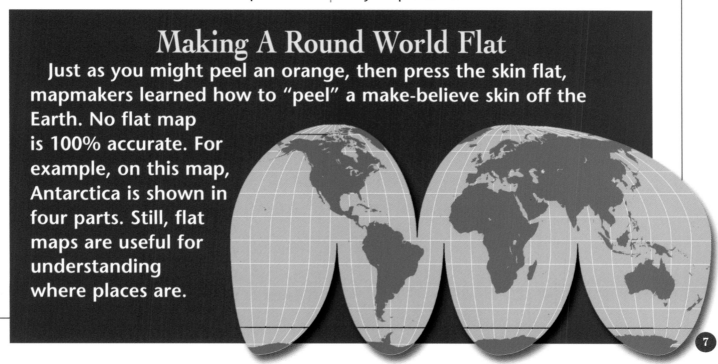

Making A Round World Flat

Just as you might peel an orange, then press the skin flat, mapmakers learned how to "peel" a make-believe skin off the Earth. No flat map is 100% accurate. For example, on this map, Antarctica is shown in four parts. Still, flat maps are useful for understanding where places are.

7 CONTINENTS
AND
5 OCEANS

• *There are seven continents and five oceans located in the world.*

Many scientists think that when the Earth was first formed, it had only one huge solid hunk of land. Over millions of years, that one big land mass split and drifted apart, giving us the **seven continents** we see on the map today. There are **five oceans** that surround the continents. Most of the Earth is covered with water.

You are about to learn about ancient Greece, Rome, and Mali—three amazing lands. You are also about to visit the first places in North America that European explorers traveled to on their journeys. Where are they? Use the map key to find these important places on this map!

NORTH AMERICA

ATLANTIC OCEAN

PACIFIC OCEAN

SOUTH AMERICA

ANTARCTICA

NORTH AMERICA
The United States is on this continent

SOUTH AMERICA
The fourth largest continent

AFRICA
The second largest continent

EUROPE
Divided from Asia by water and mountains

ASIA
The largest continent

AUSTRALIA
The smallest continent, made of many islands

PRIME MERIDIAN

The ancient Greeks were the first to divide the world into parts by drawing lines. The original Prime Meridian went through Greece. Today, it goes through England.

ARCTIC OCEAN

EUROPE

ASIA

E
F R G
S

AFRICA

PACIFIC OCEAN

M

EQUATOR

The lands along this imaginary line have days and nights that are exactly 12 hours long, 365 days a year. Read more on the next page.

INDIAN OCEAN

AUSTRALIA

SOUTHERN OCEAN

ANTARCTICA
The frozen continent

Find These Places On This Map

These places are in North America.

J	Jamestown (Virginia)
ST	St. Augustine (northern Florida)
S	San Salvador (The Bahamas)
Q	Quebec (Canada)

This place is in Africa.

| M | Mali |

These places are in Europe

E	England
R	Rome
G	Greece
F	France
S	Spain

THE WEST THE SOUTHWEST THE MIDWEST THE SOUTH

CANADA

WASHINGTON

MONTANA

NORTH DAKOTA

MINNESOTA

OREGON

IDAHO

WYOMING

SOUTH DAKOTA

WISCONSIN

MICHIGAN

NEVADA

UTAH

COLORADO

NEBRASKA

IOWA

ILLINOIS

INDIANA

OHIO

THE UNITED STATES

KANSAS

MISSOURI

KENTUCKY

CALIFORNIA

ARIZONA

NEW MEXICO

OKLAHOMA

ARKANSAS

TENNESSEE

ALABAMA

MEXICO

TEXAS

MISSISSIPPI

LOUISIANA

ALASKA   HAWAII

• *A simple letter-number grid system on maps is used to locate places.*

MAP PARTS
A CLOSER LOOK

Maps can bring us so much information. Some maps show what the Earth looks like—mountains, plains, and lakes. Other maps, like the one above, give us different information. This map helps us find the **regions** that make up the United States. There are 50 U.S. states with 48 that touch and two that do not. This map shows geographic regions.

Words To Know

- **Region**
(REE-jon)
Places that have common characteristics.

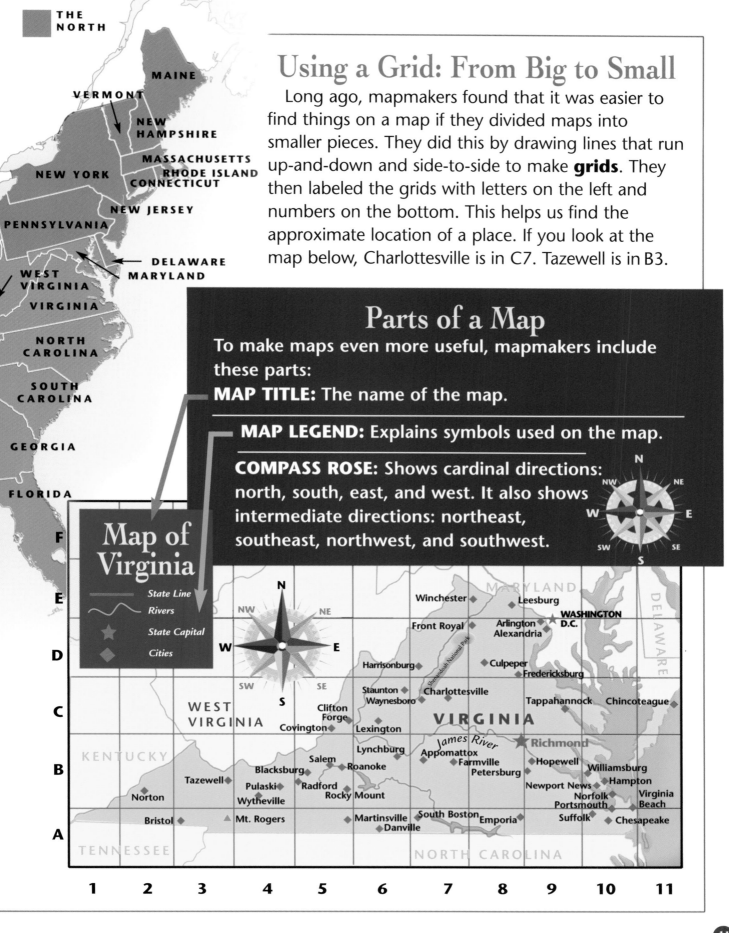

Using a Grid: From Big to Small

Long ago, mapmakers found that it was easier to find things on a map if they divided maps into smaller pieces. They did this by drawing lines that run up-and-down and side-to-side to make **grids**. They then labeled the grids with letters on the left and numbers on the bottom. This helps us find the approximate location of a place. If you look at the map below, Charlottesville is in C7. Tazewell is in B3.

Parts of a Map

To make maps even more useful, mapmakers include these parts:

MAP TITLE: The name of the map.

MAP LEGEND: Explains symbols used on the map.

COMPASS ROSE: Shows cardinal directions: north, south, east, and west. It also shows intermediate directions: northeast, southeast, northwest, and southwest.

Map of Virginia

- State Line
- Rivers
- State Capital
- Cities

LOOKING AT
OUR WORLD

• *Read and construct maps, tables, graphs, charts, and pictures to gather and display information.*

Maps are drawings of our planet, but we can also use other visual aids to tell stories about the world. What conclusions can you make after studying these different pictures, tables, charts, and graphs? Can you answer these three questions?

1. What do these regions have in common?

Pictures and charts help us classify information. This **table** uses **pictures** in rows to compare the geography of four regions. You can see that Mali is the only region with a desert.

	Ancient Greece	Ancient Rome	Empire of Mali	Virginia
Rivers		🌳	🌳	🌳
Mountains	⛰️	⛰️		⛰️
Desert			🐫	
Seas	⛵	⛵		⛵

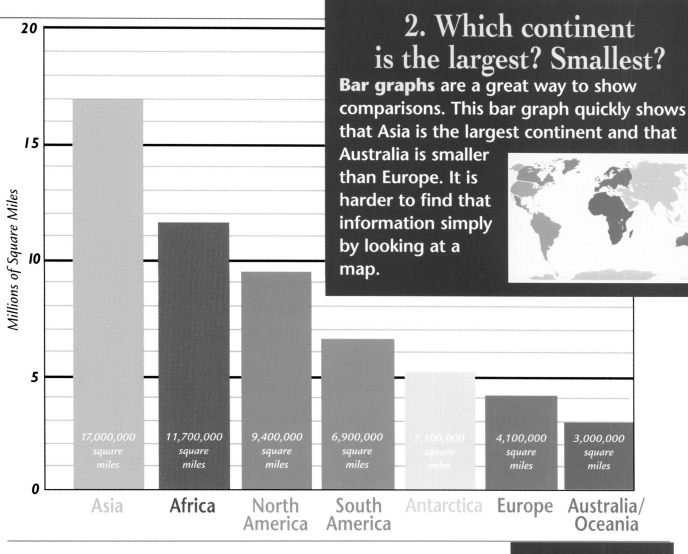

Millions of Square Miles

20

15

10

5

0

| 17,000,000 square miles | 11,700,000 square miles | 9,400,000 square miles | 6,900,000 square miles | 5,100,000 square miles | 4,100,000 square miles | 3,000,000 square miles |

Asia   **Africa**   North America   South America   Antarctica   Europe   Australia/Oceania

2. Which continent is the largest? Smallest?

Bar graphs are a great way to show comparisons. This bar graph quickly shows that Asia is the largest continent and that Australia is smaller than Europe. It is harder to find that information simply by looking at a map.

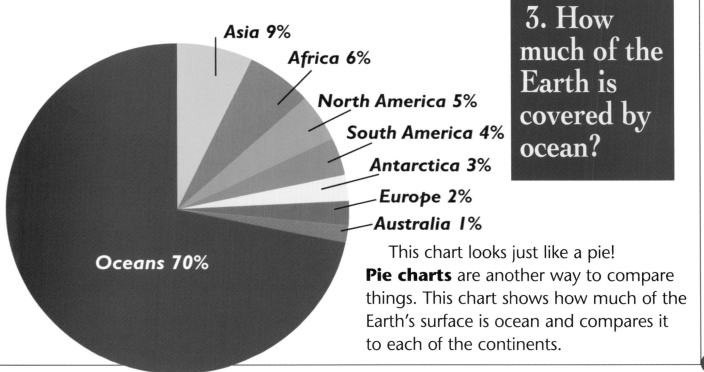

Asia 9%

Africa 6%

North America 5%

South America 4%

Antarctica 3%

Europe 2%

Australia 1%

Oceans 70%

3. How much of the Earth is covered by ocean?

This chart looks just like a pie! **Pie charts** are another way to compare things. This chart shows how much of the Earth's surface is ocean and compares it to each of the continents.

LET'S REVIEW

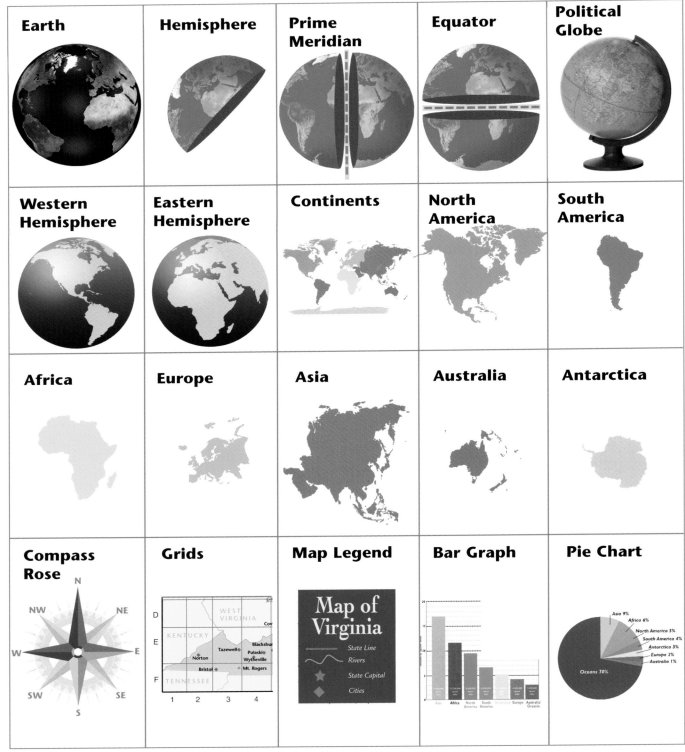

| Earth | Hemisphere | Prime Meridian | Equator | Political Globe |

| Western Hemisphere | Eastern Hemisphere | Continents | North America | South America |

| Africa | Europe | Asia | Australia | Antarctica |

| Compass Rose | Grids | Map Legend | Bar Graph | Pie Chart |

For the purposes of this review, images are not in scale.

Use pages 6-7 to answer questions 1-3.

1. What are the four hemispheres called?
2. What is a hemisphere?
3. What is the difference between the Prime Meridian and the Equator?

Use pages 8-9 to answer questions 4-6.

4. List the seven continents and five oceans.
5. On which continent are England, Spain, and France located?
6. On which continent is the United States located?

Use pages 10-11 to answer question 7 and 8.

7. Explain what kind of information these map parts give us:
   - Map title
   - Map legend
   - Compass rose

8. Use the map on page 11 with the simple letter-number grid system to locate the following places and write down each location's coordinates: Richmond; Washington, D.C.; Pulaski; Harrisonburg; Emporia.

IMAGINE IF...

- You are about to set sail from the coast of Virginia to travel around the world visiting each continent in this order: Europe, Africa, Antarctica, Australia, Asia, South America, and then back to North America. List each of the oceans you will cross on your way to each of these continents.

THINK AND DO

- Create a map of your classroom by drawing a large rectangle or square on a blank sheet of paper with the name of your classroom as the title. Draw a compass rose including the intermediate directions. Create a map legend for all the things in your classroom. For example, you may choose squares for desks, semi-circles for chairs, and triangles for windows. Draw a map of the classroom using the symbols you created.
- The pie chart on page 13 gives information about how much of the Earth is covered by water and the seven continents. Take the information from the pie chart and use the data to make it into a bar graph.

CHAPTER 2

Built almost 2,000 years ago, the Colosseum in Rome, with its many arches, was a place where great events took place—and a place that has influenced life even today, right here in Virginia.

THREE GREAT CIVILIZATIONS

Ancient Rome

The empire of Mali

Long ago and far away,
the world was a very
different place.

Explore three amazing lands
that had an impact on the
way we live our lives today.

Ancient Greece

Words To Know

- **Civilization**

  (Siv-ill-A-ZAY-shun)
  People in an advanced stage of development, with government, art, music, and public services such as running water, armies, or libraries.

- **Contributions**

  (con-trib-YOU-shunz)
  Acts of giving or doing something positive.

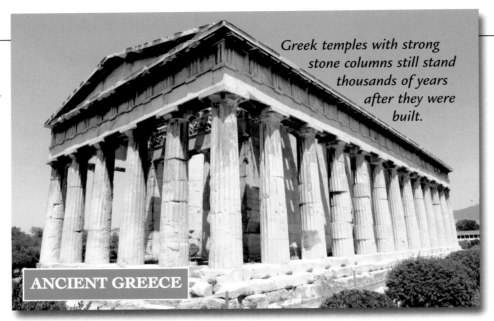

Greek temples with strong stone columns still stand thousands of years after they were built.

ANCIENT GREECE

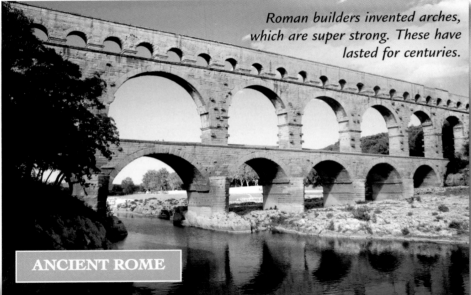

Roman builders invented arches, which are super strong. These have lasted for centuries.

ANCIENT ROME

Some of the empire of Mali's amazing buildings still stand.

EUROPE

ATLANTIC OCEAN

Rome   Greece

AFRICA

Mali

EMPIRE OF MALI

Timeline of the Past

- **The ancient Greeks and Romans were two groups of people who made significant contributions to society in terms of architecture, government, and sports.**

- **Early Mali was a wealthy trading empire before Columbus sailed to America.**

OUR WORLD
LONG AGO

Some Greek contributions: the column and beautiful artwork

A Roman contribution: the arch

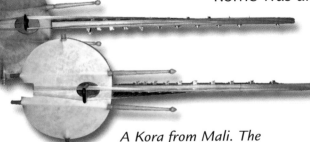

A Kora from Mali. The American banjo was influenced by it.

How can things that happened thousands of years ago still have an impact on our lives today? Three mighty **civilizations**—ancient Greece, ancient Rome, and the empire of Mali—have each made important **contributions** to the way we live right now.

We live in a land of freedom and democracy because of the ideas of ancient Greeks and Romans. We build strong bridges and buildings using designs they created more than a thousand years ago. Many of these ideas were kept safe in the great libraries of Mali in Africa at a time when Europe was living through terrible times.

Today Greece is still a country, but it is much smaller than it was long ago when it reached all the way into Asia. Today Rome is a big city in Italy, but 2,000 years ago Rome was an empire that reached into three continents.

Today Mali is a struggling country in West Africa, but a hundred years before Christopher Columbus sailed to the Americas, Mali was one of the richest and biggest empires on Earth.

Let us travel back through thousands of years and learn more about these great civilizations.

 Ancient Greece: about 1000-337 B.C.

 Ancient Rome: about 753 B.C.-300 A.D.

 The empire of Mali: about 1230-1450 A.D.

 Explorers begin crossing the oceans: 1450s

ANCIENT
GREECE

- *The ancient Greeks have influenced the lives of people today.*

Ancient
Greece

Athens

MEDITERRANEAN SEA

Words To Know

- **Column**

    (COL-um)
    A tall cylinder-shaped pillar used to support a structure.

- **Architects**

    (ARK-ih-tekts)
    People who design buildings.

- **Architecture**

    (ARK-ih-tek-chur)
    The design of buildings.

The land of Greece spreads across a group of islands and peninsulas in the Mediterranean Sea. A peninsula is a piece of land shaped like a finger with water on three sides. The Greek islands were formed when huge volcanoes exploded thousands of years ago. These islands are very rocky with many rugged mountains, but the ancient Greeks put those rocks to good use by cutting them into blocks and **columns**. They then began to build some of the most amazing buildings in the world.

Beautiful Buildings

As Greek civilization grew stronger, people began to build huge temples to honor their many gods. **Architects** used long rows of thick columns to hold up big roofs. The **Parthenon** (*PAR-the-non*) is one of the most famous examples of **architecture** on Earth. Built more than 2,400 years ago, it was a temple to honor Athena, the goddess of wisdom. It was built on a high, flat-topped hill in Athens, Greece, at a place called the Acropolis, which means "upper city."

At sunset the Parthenon and its many columns appear pink and gold. It is a beautiful sight to see.

The Parthenon has been copied many times all over the world. In fact, many of America's buildings have been inspired by Greek architecture. The building in the picture above is where America's Supreme Court meets. Our penny shows the Lincoln Memorial, which also has lots of columns. Both buildings are in Washington, D.C., where there are many other buildings designed in the Greek style.

Amazing Artwork

The Greeks loved to decorate their buildings with beautiful carvings and fancy trim. They could take hard stone and carve it into beautiful sculptures

that looked like they were made of the softest silk. Thousands of years of wear have taken a toll, but they are still beautiful.

Stone goddesses support a roof.

The Lands of Greece

● *People adapt to their environment in different ways.*

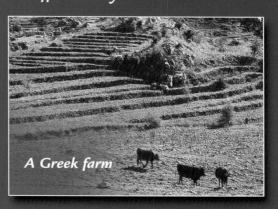

A Greek farm

Many hills and mountains made farming difficult for the ancient Greeks. They terraced the hills to farm.

A Greek island today

Greece has many islands, so merchants built ships and sailed the Mediterranean trading with other lands.

Greece's rugged mountains

Many mountains led to the development of small, independent cities.

21

Words To Know
- **Direct democracy**
A government in which people vote to make their own rules and laws.

This is a 2,000 year-old sculpture of Pericles, the man who led Athens to a true democracy.

- *Our government is based on ideas developed in ancient Greece and Rome.*

Not only did we learn the Greek way of building, we borrowed a part of the way they lived. About 2,500 years ago in the city–state of Athens, a great "experiment"—**direct democracy**—happened. That contribution changed the course of history.

Power to the People

When America broke away from England in 1776, it stopped being ruled by a king or queen who had inherited power or a ruler who took it by force. America's founders decided to try something new by borrowing something old, so they looked to ancient Greece, the birthplace of **democracy** *(dem-AH-kra-see)*. Democracy comes from the Greek word *demokratia,* which means "rule of the people."

In ancient Athens, people voted to make all their own rules and laws. The Greeks' direct democracy was not perfect. Only men could vote. Women, slaves, and people born outside of Greece could not.

Birthplace of the Olympics

Are you an athlete? That word comes from the Greek word *athlos,* which means "contest." The ancient Greeks gave us one of the best contests in the world—the Olympics. **The Olympic Games** of today were modeled after the games of ancient Greece.

It all began in 776 B.C., when a group of swift runners came to a place called Olympia as part of a religious celebration. Over the next 900 years, the number of events grew from a single foot race to include many sports.

Citizens of Athens got together to vote. People would speak about issues that were important to them. Then all the free men would say "yes" or "no" to the issue. Women could not vote.
Can you imagine how difficult it would be for everyone who can vote in America today to get together every two weeks in one place to vote?

Democracy in Ancient Greece

Every two weeks in ancient Greece, all the interested men who owned property gathered at a place near the Acropolis to discuss new ideas to make Greece a better place. They then decided "yes" or "no" to which ideas would become laws.

America's founders liked the idea of government "by the people, for the people." They, too, wanted a land where the people ruled. That great idea became an important part of our American way of life.

Sadly, a series of wars between Greece's city-states weakened the empire. Soon a new super-power arose—Rome.

This man is not throwing a frisbee. This very famous sculpture shows a discus thrower getting ready to make his toss. The discus was an Olympic sport. Today there are still throwing events in the Olympics.

In 1896 the first modern Olympics were held. Today winners hope for gold medals, but back then winners got crowns made from olive tree branches.

In 2004 the world came to Greece once more for a modern Olympics. Some events were even held at the ancient sites.

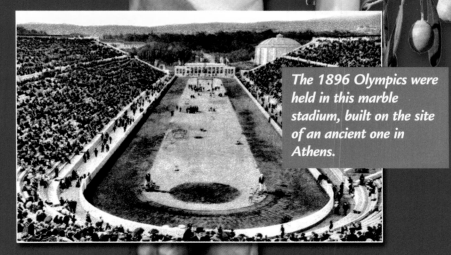

The 1896 Olympics were held in this marble stadium, built on the site of an ancient one in Athens.

23

The Lands of Rome

Olive trees

Rome is hilly and the soil is poor. The people of ancient Rome terraced their hillsides to farm.

On a Roman ship if there was no wind, men had to row.

Like the Greeks, the Romans built ships. They sailed the Mediterranean and traded with other lands.

Rome's Colosseum

The Romans were master builders, and Roman buildings still stand all across Europe.

ANCIENT ROME

EUROPE

Ancient Rome

ROME

Mediterranean Sea

AFRICA

ASIA

"All roads lead to Rome!" That was what people said at the height of the mighty Roman Empire which reached to lands as far away as Egypt. Rome was not just a city in Italy in those days. It was a huge empire that stretched into Africa and Asia. How did it get so big?

Romans on the Move

Rome's roads were masterpieces. They were good for driving chariots and wagons on and wide enough to move thousands of soldiers quickly. Those quick-stepping soldiers were the key to Rome's power. The Roman Army conquered many countries.

Everywhere they went, the ancient Romans built huge structures. Every new town they took over soon had a big sports stadium. The biggest stadium was in the city of Rome. It was called the **Colosseum** *(COL-uh-see-um),* and it was bigger and grander than many of today's modern-day stadiums.

Arches Help Build an Empire

One of Rome's greatest contributions to modern-day life is the **arch**. The Romans did not invent it, but they made the arch stronger and better and used it to build amazing bridges, monuments, and buildings.

By the year 200 A.D., more than a million people lived in Rome, and they needed water. Roman architects and engineers used arches to build huge **aqueducts** *(AH-kwi-dukts)*, which used gravity to bring water down from the mountains across broad valleys to the cities. Some are still in use today!

The Romans were master builders. They also were masters at government. Our nation's founders borrowed some Roman ideas when they were deciding how America should be run. Read all about them on the next page.

Words To Know

- **Arch**
  (artch)
  A curved stone construction that spans an opening and supports weight above it.

The Key Bridge uses arches to cross the Potomac River from Washington, D.C. to Virginia.

This ancient Roman aqueduct was built almost 2,000 years ago by Roman soldiers. The man in this photo is dressed like a Roman soldier in full armor.

25

GREAT IDEAS
FROM ROME

- *Our government is based on ideas developed in ancient Greece and Rome.*

Words To Know
- **Representative democracy**

A government in which people vote for (elect) a smaller group of citizens to represent them and to make rules and laws for everyone.

In addition to the ideas they borrowed from ancient Greece, America's founders also took contributions from ancient Rome. For about 500 years, Rome had a **republic**. That word comes from the Latin *res publica,* which means "public affairs." A republic is sometimes called a **representative** *(rep-ree-SENT-a-tiv)* **democracy** because the Romans *chose* people to represent them—people who then made the rules and laws for everyone.

Three Branches Share Power

In a monarchy *(mahn-ark-key),* the king or emperor ruled for life and made all the laws and rules. In a democracy, no one person has all the power and people serve for a fixed period of time. For example, our U.S. President serves for four years. In the Roman Republic, the *consul* (president) had the job for only one year.

We borrowed another idea. The Romans had three separate groups working together to run the country. One group wrote the laws. A second group carried out the laws, and the third group punished law-breakers. No one group had all the power, which is how we do things in the United States today!

The floor of the Colosseum no longer remains, but visitors to the ruins can see the cages where wild animals once roared.

Art and Architecture
The Romans left behind wonderful architecture and art, such as the huge **Colosseum** and paintings of Roman events.

An artist from the 1800s imagined this meeting of Rome's senate. Notice the togas the men are wearing.

The Fall of the Roman Empire

Power-hungry men with loyal soldiers to follow their commands turned Rome into a monarchy. The days of representative democracy in Rome failed.

Why did Rome's glory days end? By the year 400, Rome's empire stretched as far as Asia and Africa. It was too hard to keep control of areas that were so far away. It was also expensive to keep and feed the huge army needed to keep people from other lands under control. Under a monarchy, where power is passed from parent to child, some very bad leaders ran the country into ruin. Nations from the north attacked, and soon the Roman empire crumbled.

Augustus ended Rome's days as a republic. and declared himself Rome's first emperor, Augustus "Caeser."

At the grand opening of the Colosseum in the year 80, more than 50,000 cheering people packed its seats. Gladiators fought, comedians told jokes, and men wrestled with wild beasts! It could get bloody.

In time, a huge canvas was built to cover the top to keep out the sun and rain. The Romans even held pretend naval battles by flooding the center of the arena.

Roman artists made many images of gladiators, as well as everyday people. They created paintings, sculptures, and lots of **mosaics** (*mow-SAY-iks*) like the one on the left. Notice the thousands of tiny tile pieces.

27

THE EMPIRE OF
MALI

- *The empire of Mali was located in the western region of the continent of Africa.*

- *Early Mali was a wealthy trading empire before Columbus sailed to America.*

Words To Know

- **Caravan**

  (CARE-uh-van) A long line of camels traveling together carrying people and goods.

This 700-year-old sculpture shows a Malian soldier. Archers and horsemen were some of the most respected members of the community.

Land of Gold and Glory

Africa is a beautiful continent with many different countries. Each is as different as China is from Egypt. Africans speak different languages and have different cultures and climates. Africa was the home of several great empires and it was here, about 800 years ago, that one of the world's richest empires, the Kingdom of Mali, began its rise to glory.

Mali was one of the largest and wealthiest empires in the region, and it was **one of the most important centers of trade in the world**. That is because Mali lay across the trade routes between salt mines in the Sahara Desert and regions dotted with gold mines in West Africa.

For people of the deserts, salt was a life-saving natural resource, used both for health and keeping foods from spoiling. Salt was so valuable that it was used as money and was sometimes worth more than gold. Gold—rare, shiny, and beautiful—was also in great demand.

The Great Mosque in the city of Djenne is built in the traditional Malian way. It is made of mud! Dried mud is very strong and parts of this building are 500 years old.

Ancient Mali

AFRICA

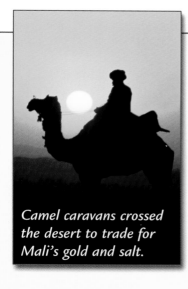

Camel caravans crossed the desert to trade for Mali's gold and salt.

A Center of Trade

Imagine a place where most people live happily. No one goes hungry. People treat one another with kindness. It is safe to walk on the streets late at night. There is music in the air and storytellers to listen to. This is what it was like in a place the people of Mali called the "Bright Country."

Salt and gold made Mali rich, and because it was so safe, long camel caravans brought all sorts of wares to the great markets. Merchants knew that they would not be robbed along the way and that folks would be honest. The buying and selling of salt and gold made Mali a crossroads of the world.

The Lands of Mali

• *People adapt to their environment in different ways.*

Caravans still cross the desert even today.

Mali has a hot climate, and people sweat a lot. Salt, a valuable natural resource, helps keep them alive.

Selling cloth in a busy market in modern Mali.

Long ago, slabs of salt were traded for gold in markets like this one.

Parts of this mosque in Mali are hundreds of years old.

There was very little stone or wood in Mali, so people built with mud. The results were amazingly beautiful.

GOLDEN
KINGDOM

- *Most of what we know about Mali's history comes from oral accounts that were handed down from Mali's storytellers.*

- *Mali was ruled by rich and powerful kings.*

Words To Know

- **Mansa Musa**

  (MAHN-suh MOO-suh)

  A famous West African king.

Salt and Gold

Today you can find salt in every supermarket, but it was not always like that. Back in the days before refrigerators, salt was the key to life. In fact, in some ways it was almost more valuable than gold.

Salt kept food from spoiling. It was used to tan leather and to make medicines. In the heat of the West African sun, where people sweat a lot, salt kept the body from losing too much water. Salt meant life, but gold, which was much-prized by Europeans, meant wealth and power!

This modern-day Malian salt seller sits next to slabs of salt that have been cut from deep beneath the ground at a salt mine.

Storytellers—Keepers of the Past

Many parts of Africa have a long tradition of storytellers called **griots** *(GREE-ohs)* or **djali** *(JAH-lee)*. These folks carried the entire history of their countries in their heads and passed traditions and stories from one generation to the next.

Storytellers were the trusted advisors of kings and queens, helping them make decisions about how to rule their lands. They were very powerful people. Today griots and djalis are still very important people in Africa, and they still tell stories about Mali's great and powerful kings, especially **Sundiata** *(Sun-JAH-tuh)* and **Mansa Musa**.

City of Learning

Mali's kings were rich, powerful men who controlled trade across West Africa. Long caravans arrived in Mali every day, bringing silks, gems, and spices from Asia and leaving with gold and salt. By the time a new king, **Mansa Musa** *(see below),* began his rule in 1307, Mali was a *very* rich empire.

Mansa Musa decided to build a great city near the Niger *(NYE-jer)* River in a place called **Timbuktu** *(Tim-buck-TOO)*. At the time, it became one of the richest cities in the world and a place devoted to learning. Mansa Musa built two great universities and more than 170 schools. Timbuktu had a great library filled with important books that held the wisdom of the world, including translations of ancient Greek and Roman books. People came from all over to study there.

End of an Empire

What happened to end all this? In time, war came to Mali, and travel became dangerous. Rival kings soon took over, but they did not rule as wisely. Soon traders began to travel by sea instead of by caravans through the desert. The schools emptied and the streets grew unsafe. A mighty empire slowly faded away.

This very old drawing shows many of Timbuktu's schools and mosques. A mosque is a Muslim place of prayer. Muslims belong to a religion known as Islam, and Mali's kings followed the Muslim faith.

Mansa Musa — Great King of Africa

Mansa Musa's throne and ball of gold.

Sundiata was Mali's first great leader, much like our George Washington. In the year 1230 he helped to free his people from an evil king and brought his country great peace.

Mansa Musa was a distant relative of Sundiata. When he took the throne, about fifty years after Sundiata died, he helped Mali grow even richer. He is known for a famous trip he took—a religious pilgrimage through Egypt to Mecca, a holy city. He gave away so much gold to poor people along the way that the value of gold dropped because it was no longer special and precious.

DIFFERENT LANDS AND LIVES

- *Every land has its own special features that affect the way people live.*
- *Ancient Greece and Rome were located near the Mediterranean Sea.*
- *The empire of Mali was located in the western region of the continent of Africa.*

Words To Know

- **Characteristics**
(cahr-ick-tuh-RIS-tix)
Different traits that describe a person or place and its size, shape, or the way it looks.

Virginia has rivers, bays, mountains, and valleys. Because of these things, we have developed all sorts of skills to help us live here. We build huge ships because the waters are important to us, and we grow crops that do well with our weather and soil. All these things make us a little different from other states.

Other lands also have their own special features. Those **characteristics** have a lot to do with the reasons each place develops the way it does.

Ancient Greece and Rome were located in and around the Mediterranean Sea. The empire of Mali sat in the western part of the continent of Africa. Each place was *very* different, yet each became great.

The land of Greece includes many islands in the Mediterranean Sea. These islands are dry and have rocky soil. Even though some are very hilly the ancient Greeks settled on them and managed to thrive.

Physical Characteristics

What was the land like in…

The Acropolis: a flat-topped hill in Athens

The Tiber River in Rome

The Niger River

ANCIENT GREECE

- A peninsula and many islands edged by the Mediterranean Sea
- Many mountains and hills
- Limited rich soil

ANCIENT ROME

- Located next to the Tiber River and near the Mediterranean Sea
- Built on many hills
- Limited rich soil

THE EMPIRE OF MALI

- Located along the Niger River in West Africa
- Mostly desert with some land for farming
- Gold and salt mines

Human Characteristics

What did the people do in…

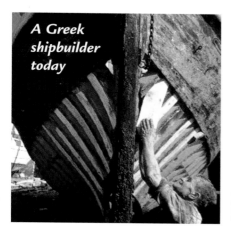

A Greek shipbuilder today

An ancient Roman road still in use today

A Mali miner today

ANCIENT GREECE

- Farmers
- Ship builders
- Traders

ANCIENT ROME

- Farmers
- Road builders
- Traders

THE EMPIRE OF MALI

- Farmers
- Miners
- Traders

LET'S REVIEW

GREECE

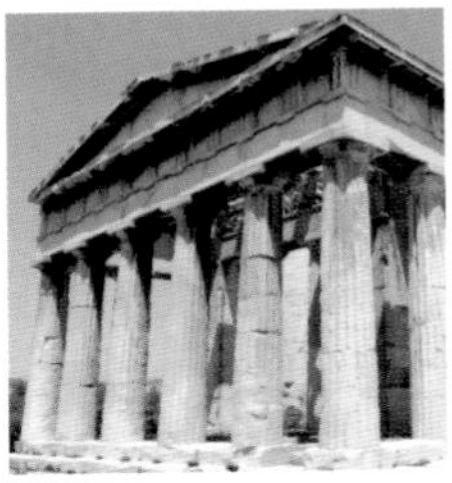
Parthenon

Columns

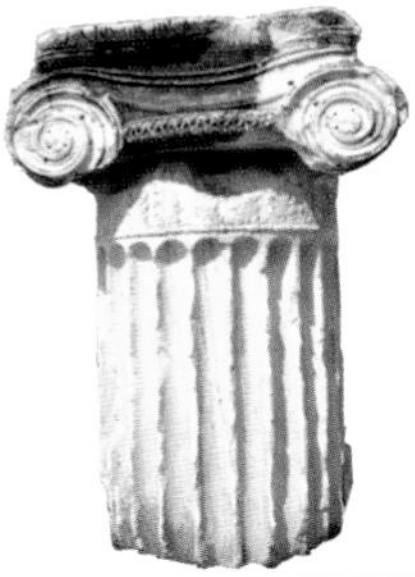

Sculpture

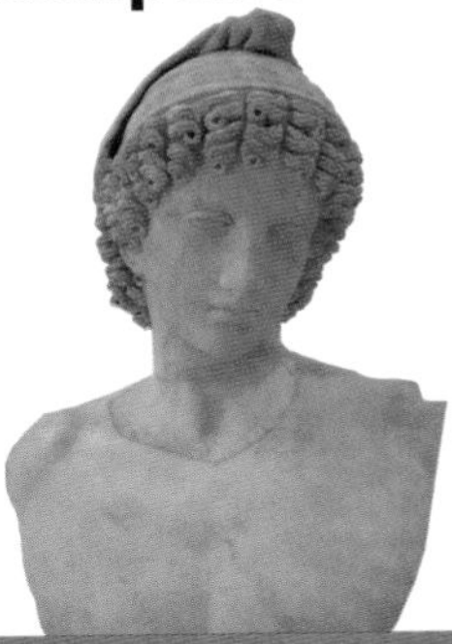

Paintings and pottery

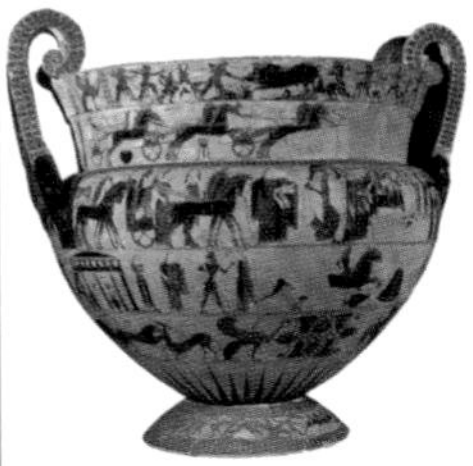

Direct Democracy

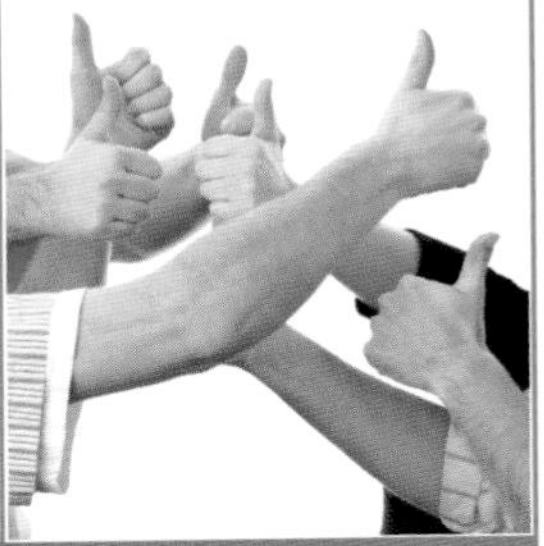

ROME

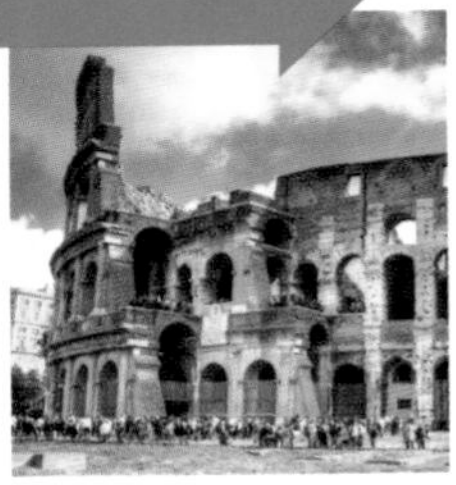
Colosseum

Arch

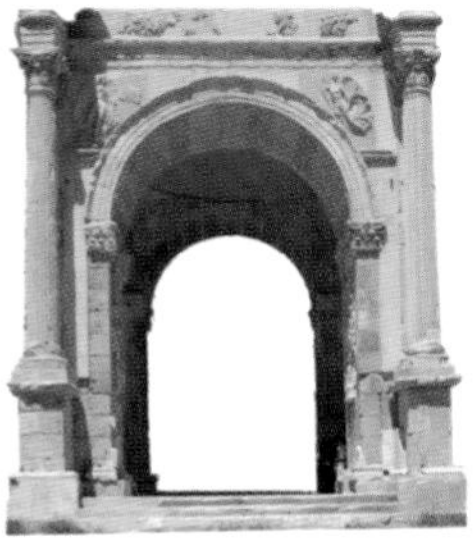

Mosaics

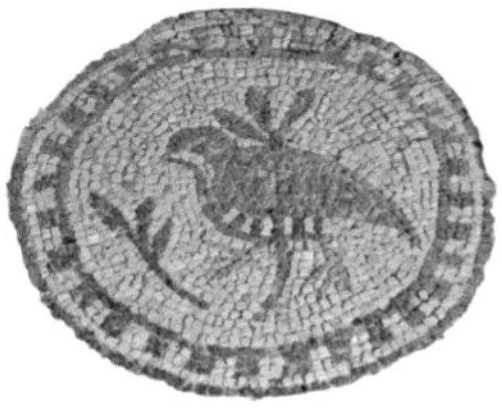

Aqueducts

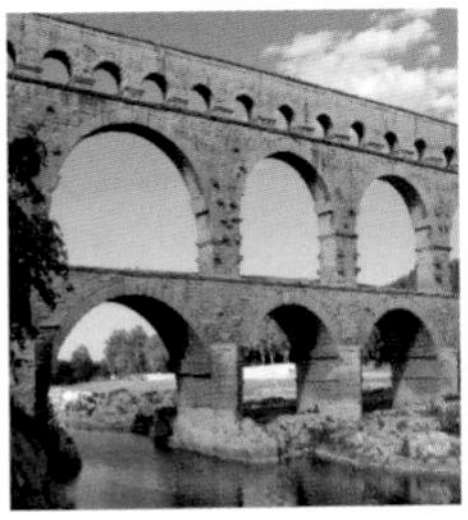

Representative Democracy

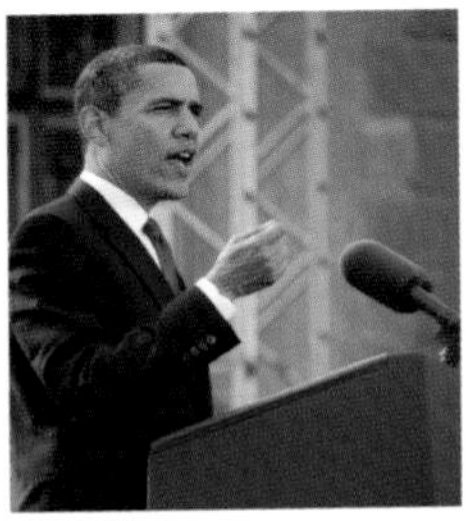

MALI

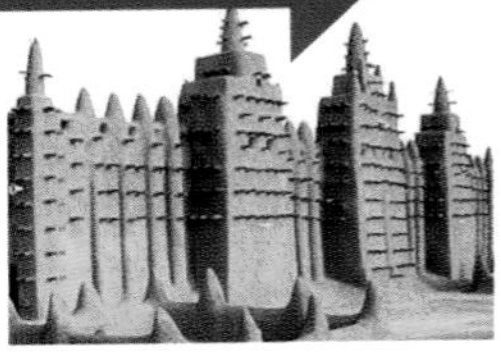
A Timbuktu mosque

Gold

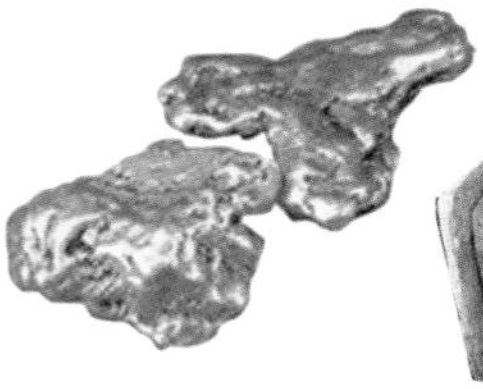

Salt

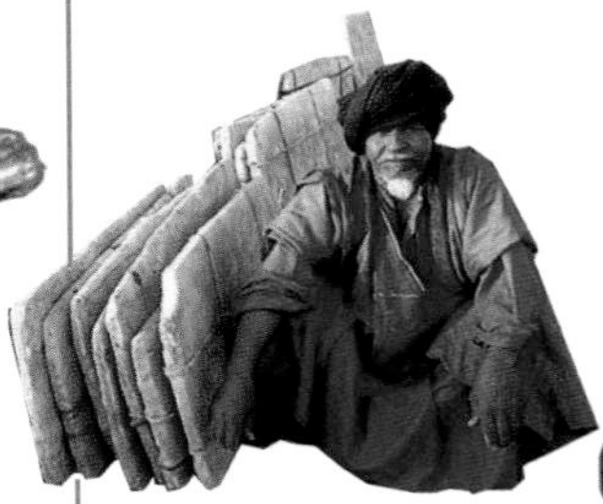

Story-teller

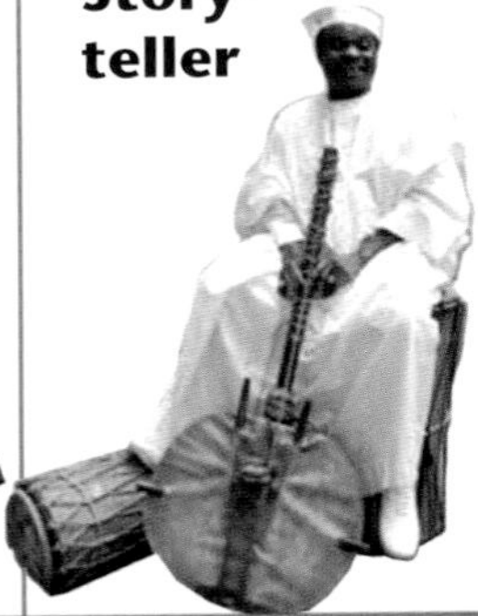

Great Libraries

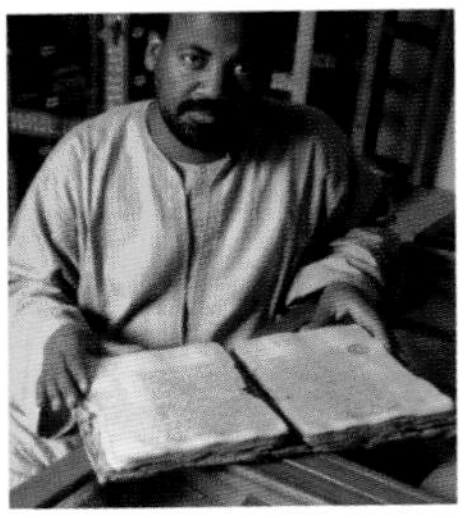

Greek characteristics	Rome characteristics	Mali characteristics
• Mediterranean Sea • Mountains and hills • Not much rich soil	• Near Mediterranean Sea and Tiber River • Very hilly • Not much rich soil	• Niger River • Mostly desert • Some rich soil for farming along the river • Gold and salt mines

Use pages 20-21 to answer questions 1-3.

1. What style of architecture came from ancient Greece?

2. What is an example of ancient Greek architecture that still exists today?

3. Name three ways the ancient Greeks adapted to their environment to meet their needs.

Use pages 22-23 to answer questions 4-6.

4. Ancient Greece's government was a direct democracy. Explain what that means.

5. What idea from ancient Greece is a part of the American government?

6. What modern sporting event came from ancient Greece?

Use pages 24-25 to answer questions 7-9.

7. What style of architecture came from ancient Rome?

8. What is an example of ancient Roman architecture that still exists today?

9. Name two ways the people of ancient Rome adapted to their environment to meet their needs.

Use pages 26-27 to answer questions 10-12.

10. Ancient Rome's government was a representative democracy. Explain what that means.

11. What two ideas of government from ancient Rome are part of our American government?

12. List three different kinds of art made by ancient Romans.

Use pages 28-29 to answer questions 13-14.

13. Why was Mali so wealthy?

14. How did the people of the empire of Mali adapt to their environment?

Use pages 30-31 to answer questions 15-17.

15. Why was salt so valuable to people living in the desert?

16. Describe the kings of the empire of Mali.

17. Why was Timbuktu an important city in Mali?

18. Why were storytellers so important in the empire of Mali?

THINK AND DO

• Choose one of the three empires in this chapter and create a poster to hang in the classroom. The poster should list and explain each of these points:

- Where was the empire located?
- What is an example of the type of architecture used by the empire?
- What kind of government ruled the empire?
- What is one interesting fact about the empire?

IMAGINE IF...

• You are a trader trekking through the Sahara with a camel caravan. Write a diary entry describing the trip. Include a description of the goods you are selling and what goods you are hoping to buy.

• You are a storyteller in the empire of Mali. Create a story about the salt and gold mines of West Africa that could have been passed down from generation to generation. After you write your story, share it verbally since this is the way storytellers shared their stories.

CHAPTER 3

Sail across scary seas to strange new lands and join in the search for riches.

An artist imagines Christopher Columbus landing on an island he named San Salvador, in the Bahamas.

THE AGE OF EXPLORATION

ACROSS A
GREAT OCEAN

- *The first explorers had different motivations, had different sponsors, and met different successes.*

This is an exact replica of the Santa Maria, *Columbus' biggest ship. It is very different from the big ships that are now built in Virginia.*

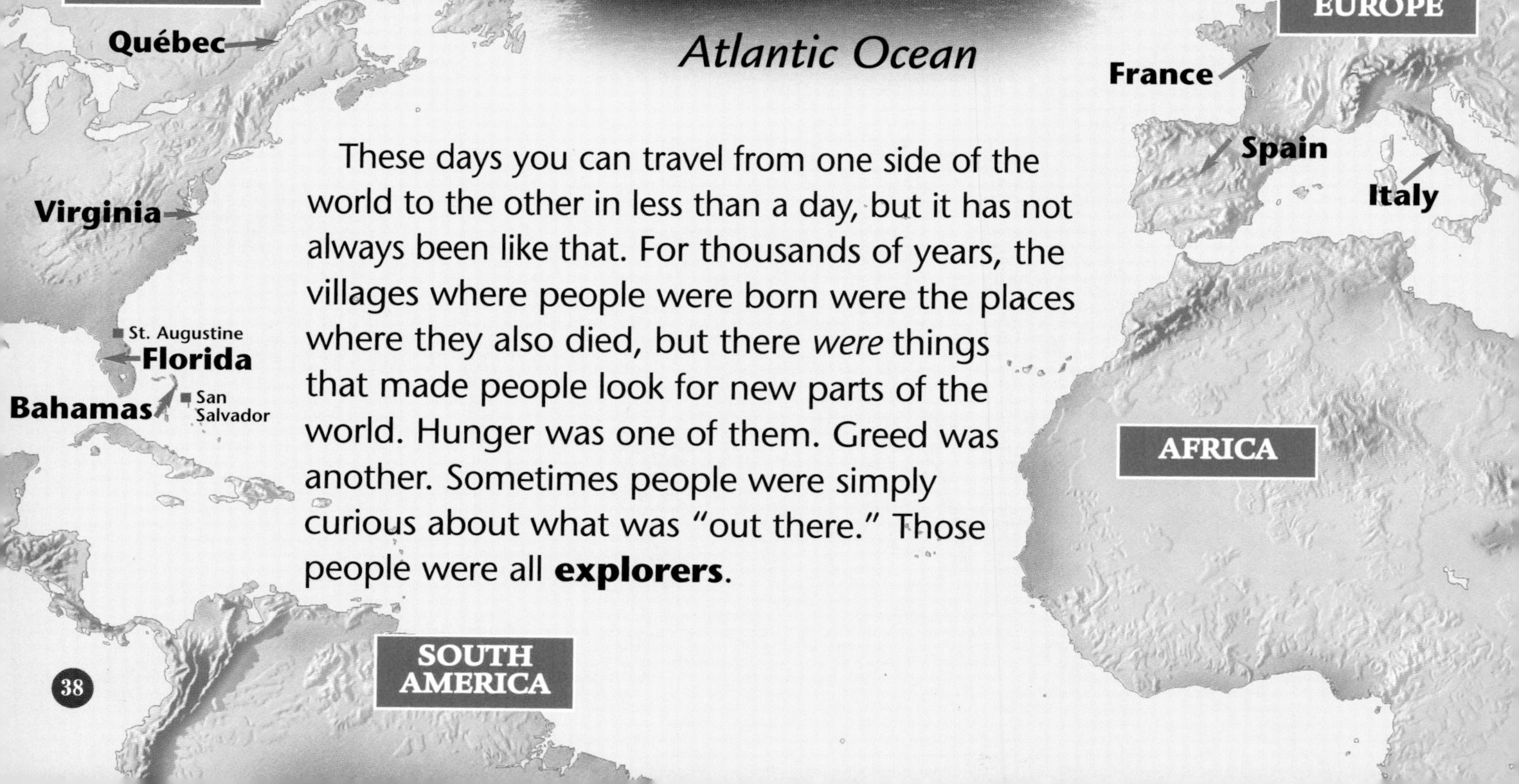

England

EUROPE

NORTH AMERICA

Québec

Atlantic Ocean

France

Spain

Italy

Virginia

These days you can travel from one side of the world to the other in less than a day, but it has not always been like that. For thousands of years, the villages where people were born were the places where they also died, but there *were* things that made people look for new parts of the world. Hunger was one of them. Greed was another. Sometimes people were simply curious about what was "out there." Those people were all **explorers**.

■ St. Augustine

Florida

Bahamas ■ San Salvador

AFRICA

SOUTH AMERICA

Ancient Explorers

As far back as ancient Egypt, people were visiting unknown lands, usually with the idea of taking them over. The ancient Chinese were great explorers, but the **Europeans**, starting with the Greeks and Romans, had the greatest need to push beyond their boundaries. Their early explorers went east and met people from other lands who had things that they did not have—things like gold, silver, and silks. Asians had something the Europeans *really* wanted—spices. Spices grew in the Indies, which is a part of Asia, and helped mask the taste of spoiling food in the days before refrigerators.

Danger Ahead!

For many years traders brought the riches of Asia to Europe, but in the mid 1400s wars broke out and travel became too dangerous. It became difficult to travel *east* to get spices, so a few bold folks decided to try sailing across the great ocean to the *west*. Europe's first explorers did not know how big that mysterious ocean—the Atlantic Ocean—was or that they would accidently find a huge continent. That did not stop them from trying.

"Where Am I and Who Are You?"

The explorers made a lot of mistakes! They hoped the Atlantic Ocean was small, but their trips took months. When they finally reached land, some of them thought they were in the Indies, so they called the people living there Indians. When they realized they had landed on a "new" continent, they kept trying to find a passage—perhaps a river—that would cut across it and bring them to Asia.

Hundreds of explorers dreamed of becoming rich by finding new lands, but exploring was dangerous work, and many died.

Words To Know

- **Explorer**
  (ex-PLORE-ur)
  A person who travels seeking new discoveries.

- **European**
  (Your-a-PEA-in)
  A person from one of the countries in Europe.

Marco Polo was an explorer from Venice (in what is now Italy). He made a famous trip by land to China and the Indies. He returned with many stories. His tales inspired others to try to get to Asia.

CHRISTOPHER
COLUMBUS

- *First European to discover a direct sea route to America*

- *"Discovered" the Western Hemisphere with his landing on an island that he named San Salvador*

Columbus made four voyages to the New World. Match the color with the lines on the map to see where he went each time.

| 1st voyage |
| 2nd voyage |
| 3rd voyage |
| 4th voyage |

Sailing West

On the morning of August 3, 1492, Christopher Columbus, an Italian sailing for Spain, set off to do something no one had done before. Like most educated people of his day, Columbus knew the world was round. He hoped to reach Asia by sailing west across the great sea that rimmed Europe. The only thing he did not know was how big that ocean, the Atlantic, was.

He convinced the King and Queen of Spain, Ferdinand and Isabella, to pay for his trip by promising to give Spain any lands and treasures he found. In return, they gave him three ships—the **Niña**; the **Pinta**; and a cargo ship, the **Santa Maria**.

His fleet covered only about 150 miles a day. The trip dragged on, and his crew grew scared. Finally on the 70th day of their journey, they spotted land. Columbus thought he had reached the Indies, so he called the natives "Indians." In truth he had landed on an island in what is now the Bahamas, and he named it San Salvador.

He did not find gold on his first voyage, although on later trips he did. Instead he found a new land for Spain to explore. Columbus was not the first person from Europe to "discover" America, but he opened a path between Europe and the Western Hemisphere and changed life forever for both.

JUAN
PONCE DE LEÓN

- *First European to land in Florida (near St. Augustine)*
- *Claimed the land of Florida for Spain*

"Give Me Your Gold!"

One of the men on Columbus's second voyage was a Spanish soldier who dreamed of getting rich—Juan Ponce de León. He stayed in the Americas and made a fortune mining gold, trading slaves, and stealing land. In 1508 he conquered what is now Puerto Rico and became its governor, but because he was so cruel, he was pushed out of office.

In April of 1513 Ponce de León became the first European to land on the mainland of what would one day become the United States. Legends tell us that he sailed to Florida to look for the *Fountain of Youth*—a magical spring that would give eternal life to anyone who drank from it. All he *really* wanted was more gold, more slaves, and more land to govern. He named the land he found *Pascua de Florida,* which means "feast of flowers," and claimed it for Spain. He also explored an area that would one day be called St. Augustine, but he did not find gold, so Ponce de León kept looking.

In 1521 he returned to Florida to explore its west coast. His ship was met by natives with bows and poisoned arrows. Ponce de León was shot and soon died from his wounds, but he gave Europe its first settlement in what was to become the United States of America.

There have been many stories about the Fountain of Youth. An artist painted this imaginative scene of Ponce de León and his men landing in Florida and testing the waters.

There was no Fountain of Youth, but Ponce de León's first fort still stands in St. Augustine, Florida.

Ponce de León's explorations

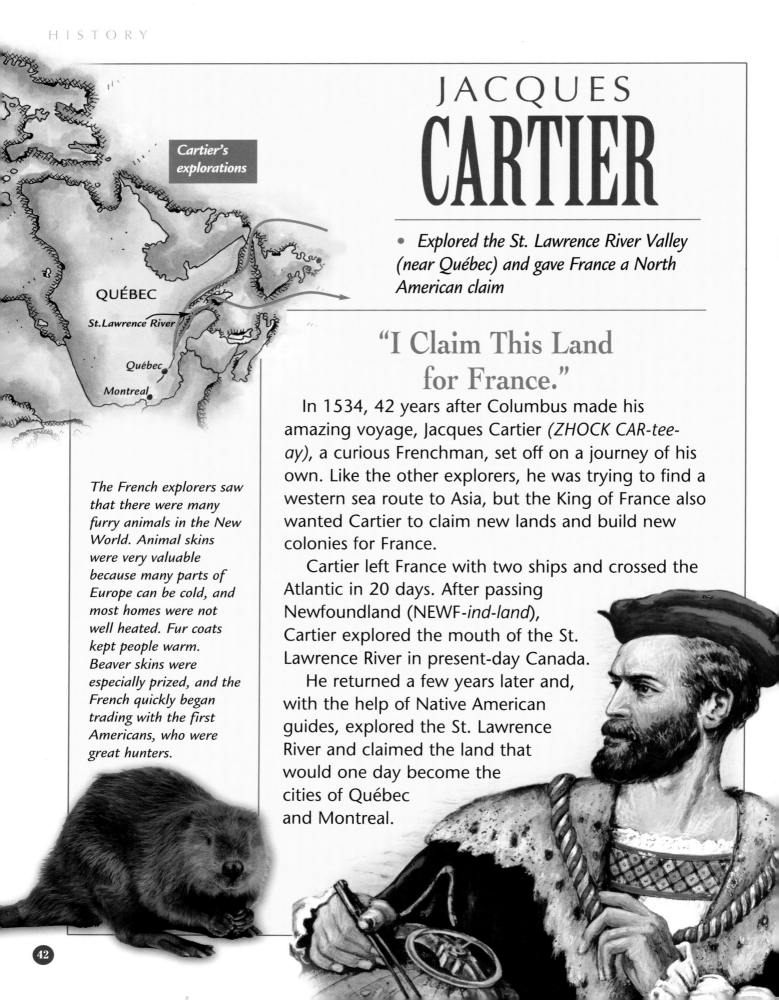

Cartier's explorations

QUÉBEC

St. Lawrence River

Québec

Montreal

JACQUES CARTIER

- *Explored the St. Lawrence River Valley (near Québec) and gave France a North American claim*

"I Claim This Land for France."

In 1534, 42 years after Columbus made his amazing voyage, Jacques Cartier *(ZHOCK CAR-tee-ay)*, a curious Frenchman, set off on a journey of his own. Like the other explorers, he was trying to find a western sea route to Asia, but the King of France also wanted Cartier to claim new lands and build new colonies for France.

Cartier left France with two ships and crossed the Atlantic in 20 days. After passing Newfoundland *(NEWF-ind-land)*, Cartier explored the mouth of the St. Lawrence River in present-day Canada.

He returned a few years later and, with the help of Native American guides, explored the St. Lawrence River and claimed the land that would one day become the cities of Québec and Montreal.

The French explorers saw that there were many furry animals in the New World. Animal skins were very valuable because many parts of Europe can be cold, and most homes were not well heated. Fur coats kept people warm. Beaver skins were especially prized, and the French quickly began trading with the first Americans, who were great hunters.

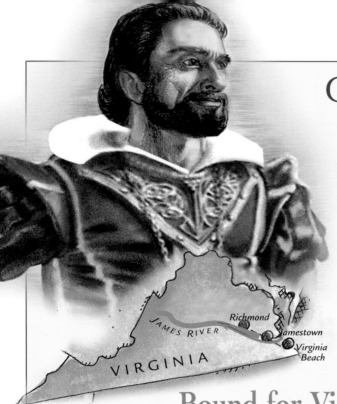

CHRISTOPHER NEWPORT

- *Brought the first colonists to Jamestown, Virginia, and made four more voyages to America*

- *One of the first Europeans to explore the James River*

Bound for Virginia

King James of England knew other countries were starting colonies in the New World. He, too, was eager to start new colonies, and to find riches and a western route to Asia. In 1605 he hired Christopher Newport to explore the North American coast to search for a good spot to build.

On a frosty December day in 1606, Captain Newport set sail for America aboard the *Susan Constant.* Two other ships joined his fleet. The three boats carried more than 100 men and boys who hoped to start the first permanent English colony in America. They landed on a swampy peninsula in Virginia, built a fort, and called it Jamestown, in honor of their king.

Newport explored the waters around Jamestown by sailing up the river he also named after King James. He reached the river's fall line—rapids near the western edge of the coastal plain—in what is now Richmond. Aboard Newport's ship were a group of "gentlemen" who were ill-suited for the harsh life in the new colony. Most did not survive, but Newport made four more trips to North America in search of riches and a route west to Asia. He found neither but played a big role in Virginia's history.

This is an exact replica of the HMS Susan Constant, *the ship that Christopher Newport sailed on his first trip to Virginia.*

• *Due to European explorations, American Indians experienced changes to their culture and their environment.*

A child learns to make beads as his father works by firelight. Loving families would soon be torn apart by the arrival of the settlers from Europe.

WHEN AMERICAN INDIANS AND EUROPEANS MET:
A TERRIBLE TIME

Mine. All Mine.

Imagine this. Strangers arrive on your doorstep. They are tired and hungry. Some are sick. You invite them in and give them food. Soon they start taking your things. They push you out of your bedroom, and soon they push you out of your house. How would you feel?

That is what often happened all across America whenever European explorers and settlers met with American Indians.

500 Nations

European explorers bragged about "discovering" America, but the truth is there were millions of people living in over 500 different nations in the Americas on the day the first European ships dropped their anchors along the Atlantic coast. The first people of the Americas lived all across the continent, in woodlands and grasslands, from the chilly north to the warm southwest. American Indians lived in thousands of towns and villages, each with strong cultures, languages, and traditions. All that changed with the arrival of the Europeans.

Pushed From Their Homelands

The kings and queens of Europe who paid for the explorers' trips wanted gold and land. Their explorations led to new settlements in the Americas as land was "claimed" in the name of Spain, France, England, and other European countries. Armed with guns, cannons, and sometimes attack dogs, the European settlers quickly began to grab what was not theirs. They tried to enslave the Indians and force European religious beliefs on them. It was a very sad time, and the American Indians were soon forced to leave their homelands and relocate to other regions.

The first European settlers at Jamestown landed with guns ready to fire.

Death by Fever

One of the deadliest blows to strike the American Indians did not come from guns or attack dogs. This "weapon" could not be seen. It traveled through the air in sneezes and coughs and on clothes and blankets. Unseen germs caused terrible diseases such as smallpox and measles, which could quickly wipe out entire Indian villages.

A healer tries to save a dying man with prayers and herbs.

Why did this happen? The peoples of the Americas had never been exposed to these germs before and had no immunity. That meant their bodies could not fight off the germs. Three out of every four American Indians on the continent died.

Entire communities perished along with their histories and traditions. With no warriors to protect the lands, newcomers from Europe could simply move in and take over.

LET'S REVIEW

EXPLORER	COUNTRY OR SPONSOR	REASON FOR EXPLORING	SUCCESSES/ ACHIEVEMENTS
CHRISTOPHER COLUMBUS	SPAIN · Born in Genoa	• *To find a western sea route to Asia*	• First European to discover a sea route to America • "Discovered" the Western Hemisphere • Landed at San Salvador, Bahamas
JUAN PONCE DE LEÓN	SPAIN	• *To discover riches* • *To conquer new lands*	• First European to land in Florida (near St. Augustine) • Gave Spain claim to Florida
JACQUES CARTIER	FRANCE	• *To colonize the Americas*	• Explored the St. Lawrence River Valley (in what is now Quebec, Canada) • Gave France a North American claim
CHRISTOPHER NEWPORT	ENGLAND	• *To discover riches* • *To find a western route to Asia* • *To colonize Virginia*	• Arrived at what is now present-day Jamestown, Virginia • Made four more journeys to start colonies in Jamestown • First to reach the James River Fall Line

REVIEW QUESTIONS

Use page 39 to answer question 1.

1. What is the difference between an explorer and a European? Do you have to be European to be an explorer?

Use pages 40-43 to answer questions 2-3.

2. List the reasons why each person wanted to be an explorer.
    - Christopher Columbus (p. 40)
    - Juan Ponce de León (p. 41)
    - Jacques Cartier (p. 42)
    - Christopher Newport (p. 43)

3. In one or two sentences explain the successes and achievements of each early European explorer.
    - Christopher Columbus (p. 40)
    - Juan Ponce de León (p. 41)
    - Jacques Cartier (p. 42)
    - Christopher Newport (p. 43)

Use pages 44-45 to answer question 4.

4. What were the three main effects of European explorations on American Indians?

THINK AND DO

- Pretend you are Christopher Columbus and write a diary entry for the day you landed in the Americas. Be sure to include what you may have seen, heard, and felt as you took your first steps in the New World.

IMAGINE IF...

- Imagine you have the chance to be a deckhand on a ship captained by Columbus, Ponce de León, Cartier, or Newport. Which explorer would you choose to sail with and why?

- Imagine that you are a young American Indian watching the first European explorers in America for the first time. How would you describe these strangers? How do you think you would feel towards them? Why do you think you would feel this way?

- Imagine if Ponce de León had found a Fountain of Youth. How different do you think the world would be today and why?

OUR ECONOMY

We depend on our resources to survive.

How do we use the Earth's limited resources to survive and prosper?

How did people in the past do the same?

Many places where ancient markets were held are still used today.

THE WORLD'S
RESOURCES

- *Resources are used to produce goods and services.*
- *Producers of goods and services are influenced by natural, human, and capital resources.*

Words To Know

- **Natural resources**
Useful materials that come directly from nature.

- **Human resources**
People working to produce goods and services.

- **Capital resources**
Goods made by people and used to produce other goods and services.

The next time you eat a bowl of cereal, think about what goes into making and selling those flakes, puffs, or pops. There are **natural resources**—the wheat the cereal is made from and the trees that were cut down to make paper for the box. There are **human resources**—farmers who grow the wheat, people who bake the flakes, the designers who create the box art, and the cashier who rings up your purchase. There are **capital resources**—machines that cut the wheat, factories where the flakes are made, trucks that bring the boxes of cereal to grocery stores, and so much more. Everything is connected!

Natural resources (sand), human resources (drivers and engineers), and capital resources (machines) are all busy working together.

Natural Resources—Nature's Basics

WOOD
- Used to build houses, produce paper, make cardboard boxes, and more!

COAL
- Used to make steel, produce electricity, make plastics, and more!

WATER AND SOIL
- Both are needed to grow crops. Water is also used to make electricity and more!

Human Resources—People

PEOPLE MAKING THINGS (GOODS)
- Factory workers, construction workers, textile workers, artists, and more!

PEOPLE HELPING PEOPLE (SERVICES)
- Teachers, doctors, nurses, lawyers, barbers, mechanics, musicians, waiters, police, and more!

Capital Resources—Tools and Machines

MACHINES
- Things that do work: bulldozers, computers, lawn mowers, and more!

TOOLS
- Things to help you do a job: hammers, nails, rakes, and more!

BUILDINGS
- Places to work: fire houses, stores, factories, hospitals, and more!

- *Ancient Greece and Rome had access to the sea (natural resource), so they used their human and capital resources to produce ships (goods), which they used for transportation (service) in trading.*

- *Mali used human and capital resources to mine gold (natural resource).*

Words To Know

- ### Producers
  (Pro-DOO-sirs)
  People who use resources to make goods and/or provide services.

- ### Goods
  Things that people make or use to satisfy needs and wants.

- ### Services
  Activities that satisfy people's needs and wants.

LIVING IN THE
ANCIENT WORLD

The people of ancient Greece, Rome, and Mali were just like us. They got hungry and needed food. They liked nice clothing. They needed tools to fish and farm. They were **producers** who used their resources to make **goods** or provide **services**—the things and activities they needed to survive and live happily.

Each empire had to cope with a different geography, from mountains to deserts to the oceans and rivers that shape life. As a result, each land's wants and needs were different too.

Do You Want It or Need It?

People everywhere **need** basic food, clothing, and shelter from the weather. Most people also **want** nice things too, such as toys, jewelry, and sweets to eat.

How did ancient empires fill their wants and needs? Greece, Rome, and Mali had different ways of providing services to help people get what they wanted.

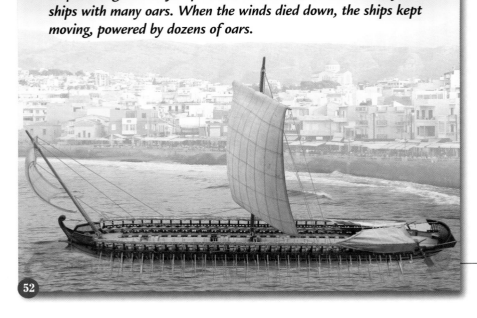

Shipbuilding was very important to the ancient Greeks. They built ships with many oars. When the winds died down, the ships kept moving, powered by dozens of oars.

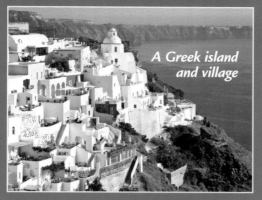

Much of Greece is on a peninsula. It has many mountains and hills and lots of small islands in the Mediterranean Sea.

A bridge over the Tiber River

Many parts of the Roman empire were also on the Mediterranean, but its capital city, Rome, was built along the Tiber River.

A present day Mali gold mine

The empire of Mali was in West Africa. Mali's kings controlled many gold mines.

Greece: Tied to the Sea

Because of their closeness to the sea, the ancient Greeks were master shipbuilders. They fished a lot but only had limited rich soil to farm. They grew olives and grapes and made oils and wine. They also made beautiful pottery to hold the bounty of the land.

A Greek urn shows people picking olives. Grapes were another big crop.

Rome: From Tree to Boat

Like Greece, Rome had limited good soil for farming, but many kinds of trees. The Romans used those trees to build ships. Then they sailed to parts of Asia and Africa to trade their goods, such as grapes and olives. They, too, made wonderful pottery to hold their food and drink. Most people survived by fishing or farming.

An ancient mosaic shows two Roman fishermen.

Mali: Treasure from Below

Mali's greatest resource was gold. People do not need gold to survive, but many people want it. Gold was in great demand in Europe. Some Malians worked in the gold and salt mines digging for these very precious things. The people of Mali then traded gold for salt, and traded both with people from Europe, Asia, and Africa.

This hunk of ore has veins of gold running through it.

Specialization in Virginia: People Doing What They Do Best

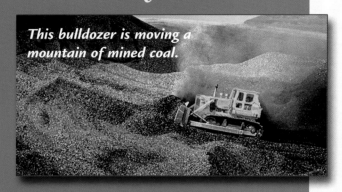

This bulldozer is moving a mountain of mined coal.

What do the people of Virginia do well? In Virginia, we have a long ocean coastline in the east. We have mountains in the west filled with coal. Those are some of the things that make our state **special**. As a result, we specialize in building boats and mining coal.

Trains loaded with coal at the Norfolk docks

Coal from the western part of Virginia travels by train to ports on the Atlantic coast. There the coal is loaded onto boats and sold all over the world.

LET'S TRADE

- *People and regions specialize because they cannot produce everything they want.*

- *People trade for things they need and want but do not have.*

Often geography plays a big role in what a person or company can produce. Think about it. People who live in deserts with no rivers, or inland far from the ocean, are not going to be good at building boats. If you live in a place surrounded by water, you will *need* boats. Soon you might open a shipyard. Then you will need to hire people with special skills to build and repair the boats. When all this happens, you have become specialized. People and regions often specialize in the production of certain goods and services.

Why Do People Trade?

The aircraft carrier *USS Harry S. Truman* (shown right), was built in Newport News, a city with a **specialization** in building boats. Even though we build these huge ships, we still depend on goods and services that come from other parts of the world to make them. These days many big ships are made from steel. There are no big steel mills in Virginia, so we get our steel from someplace else. We also have to buy other materials needed to make ships.

The buying and selling of things to produce goods and services is sometimes known as **trade**.

What's Good About Trade?

What happens when you need something that cannot be made or found where you live? Specialization leads to trade because people want goods and services they do not have.

A car maker needs steel to build trucks and automobiles, but steel workers need cars to get to their jobs. People who live in big cities need fresh fruit and vegetables. Farmers who grow fruits and vegetables need machines made in factories.

Virginia has coal mines, so we sell coal to other states and countries, but we do not produce much oil to heat our homes or gas to run our cars. We must buy oil and gas from other places. We rely on others for many of the things we need to live. We trade our ships and coal for the things we cannot make here in Virginia, and everyone benefits.

Words To Know

- ### Specialization
  (Spesh-uh-li-ZAY-shun)

  What occurs when people focus on the production of selected goods and services.

If you own a car, but you do not have gasoline, your car will not take you anywhere. Some regions specialize in making cars, others in drilling for gas and oil. The two regions need each other. They must trade.

The amazing Virginia-built aircraft carrier, USS Harry S. Truman, is longer than three football fields! Virginia specializes in building ships.

MAKING CHOICES

- *People make choices because they cannot have everything they want.*

- *All choices require giving something up (opportunity cost).*

Do you get an allowance? Have you ever received a birthday card with money tucked in it? It is nice to have all that money, but it is sometimes hard to decide what to spend it on. There are so many good things to do with it! You have to make an **economic choice** and decide what to do.

One Big Thing?

Some items cost a lot, such as the hottest new video games. You could buy lots and lots of candy for the price of one game, but the candy will not last, while you will have the game for a long time. You might save your money for something really big, such as a new bike or a nifty skateboard. Or you could give some of your money to charity and help someone needy.

What economic choice would you make? Sometimes it is not easy since many choices require giving something else up!

This boy has made a choice to give some of his money to charity instead of spending it.

"I Can't Decide"

Imagine that you have just received $20 and have gone to a big toy store to spend it. You have to make an economic choice. You would like a new set of Legos™, but you are also tempted by a brand-new DVD of a movie you love.

You have to compare the two. If you buy the DVD, you will lose the **opportunity** to build cool things with the blocks. This is called the **opportunity cost**. If you choose the blocks, you will miss the opportunity to watch that great movie. What would *you* buy?

One girl bought popcorn. The other chose ice cream. One way they can have a bit of both is if they share!

Making Economic Choices

CHOICES	CHOICES MADE	CHOICES GIVEN UP
Ice Cream or Popcorn?	Ice Cream	Popcorn
Toy or favorite DVD?	Toy	Favorite DVD
Spend it now or save for the future?	Spend it now	Save for the future

LET'S REVIEW

Natural Resource

Human Resource

Capital Resource

Producer

Goods

Services

Ancient Greece:
Natural Resources:
• olives, grapes, fish
Human Resources:
• shipbuilders, farmers, fishermen
Capital Resources:
• ships

Ancient Rome:
Natural Resources:
• olives, grapes, rivers
Human Resources:
• road builders, farmers, soldiers
Capital Resources:
• aqueducts

Ancient Mali:
Natural Resources:
• gold, salt
Human Resources:
• miners
Capital Resources:
• marketplaces
• library

Specialization

Trade

Economic choice

Opportunity cost

Use pages 50-51 to answer question 1.
1. Copy and complete the chart on a separate sheet of paper.

ECONOMIC RESOURCES	EXAMPLES	HOW ARE THEY USED?
Natural		
Human		
Capital		

Use page 52 to answer question 2.
2. Give one example of how a producer can use a natural, human or capital resource to produce a good or service?

Use pages 52-53 to answer questions 3-5.
3. West African empire of Mali
- Where was it located?
- What was a natural resource found there?
- What goods and services did human resources help to produce?

4. Ancient Greece
- Where was it located?
- What were its natural resources?
- What goods and services did human resources help to produce?

5. Ancient Rome
- Where was it located?
- What were its natural resources?
- What goods and services did human resources help to produce?

Use pages 54-55 to answer questions 6 and 7.
6. Why do people who specialize have to depend on others?
7. Why do people trade?

Use pages 56-57 to answer questions 8 and 9.
8. Why does an economic choice mean that you have to give up something?
9. What do you call the choice you give up when you make an economic choice?

THINK AND DO

- Create a list of all the games, toys, food, and anything else that you want for your birthday. Your parents have said that you can only have three of those things. Make a list of your economic choices and a list of the opportunity costs.

- Think about one thing your school needs. Make a list of all the natural, human, and capital resources it would take in order for your school to have it. After the list is done, write a letter to the principal explaining why you think it is important for the school to have this and what resources would be needed.

CHAPTER 5

OUR GREAT COUNTRY

Find out how our government keeps us safe and secure.

The Virginia Capitol in Richmond

Mount Rushmore—a huge stone monument in South Dakota—honors four of our Presidents: George Washington, Thomas Jefferson, Theodore Roosevelt, and Abraham Lincoln.

AMERICA'S GOVERNMENT

- *Governments protect the rights and property of individuals.*

- *Governments exist at the local (community), state (Virginia), and national (United States) levels.*

By the People, For the People

No matter where we live, be it a big city or tiny town, we work hard to keep our **communities** safe. We help our neighbors and lend a hand when someone needs one. We try to treat people fairly, follow the rules, and obey the laws. What exactly is a law? Who makes the laws?

Rules are things that people must or must not do. You *must* not hit others. You *must* not steal. **Laws** are written rules by which people live. You *must* stop at a red light. You *must* wear a seatbelt. Rules and laws keep us safe and help maintain order. They are made by our **government**, the people we have chosen to make the rules and laws that help keep us safe.

Our government also carries out those laws and decides if they have been broken. If the laws *are* broken, our government sees to it that the law-breakers are punished fairly. It is a big job, and because it is so complex, there are several different levels of government, some big and some small.

Words To Know

- **Communities**
Places where people live, work, and play.

- **Rules**
What people must or must not do.

- **Laws**
Important rules written and carried out by the government.

- **Government**
A group of people who makes rules and laws, carries out rules and laws, and decides if rules and laws have been broken.

Our National Government

Running the entire country is a huge job. The people who work for our nation's government must make sure that the laws of our nation are carried out. The President of the United States is the highest ranking person in government.

Our government keeps us safe from harm with the Army, Navy, Air Force, and Marine Corps. They also keep interstate highways in good shape, print money, make sure our nation's resources are used wisely, and collect taxes that are used to pay for all of the things they do. Washington, D.C. is our nation's capital.

Our State Government

In addition to the national government, each state has a government too. Our state capital is in Richmond. What decisions get made there? Plenty! The Governor of Virginia is in charge of many things. Virginia's government is in charge of public schools and universities. They issue driver's licenses and register cars. Many roads fall under the care of the state as well. Public health is another state concern, and state workers make sure restaurants are clean and that our water is healthy.

Our Local Government

In addition to national and state governments, we have a government close to home. Local governments run our counties, cities, and towns. They run public schools, parks, and community centers. They must have police departments, fire stations, and crews to take care of local roads. Being a mayor or running a county can be a busy job!

Three Different Levels of Government

At the United States Capitol laws for the entire country are made.

The governor runs Virginia from the state capitol in Richmond.

Local governments have city halls like this one in Chesapeake, Virginia.

WE, THE
PEOPLE

- *Some basic principles held by American citizens include the right to life, liberty, the pursuit of happiness, and equality under the law.*

In 1776, after a long fight with Britain over unfair taxes, the American colonists got fed up. America's smartest, boldest citizens got together and made a list of the reasons why the colonies should separate from Britain. The document that spelled out those reasons was called the **Declaration of Independence**, and it promised the new Americans "life, liberty, and the pursuit of happiness."

All Men Are Created Equal

The new Americans were also promised **equality** under the law. That means that we must all have the same chances to learn, get jobs, and have a safe place to live. No one can take those rights—the freedoms with which we are all born—away from us!

All this freedom sounds like a great idea, but if there were no laws at all, life might be dangerous. We needed rules, so America's great thinkers got together and tried to write a plan of government for our nation.

Life, Liberty, and Happiness: What Do They Really Mean?

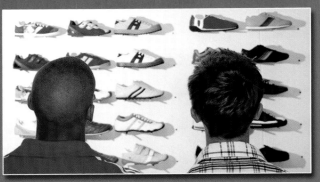

LIFE means that we must all live in safety. One way our government pursues life is by protecting us from harm with armed forces that stand ready to defend our country.

LIBERTY is the freedom to make choices. Pursue liberty by thinking, feeling, or choosing as you please as long as it does not hurt others.

America's first try, the **Articles of Confederation**, did not work. There was no way for the new government to collect money for an army. States with a lot of people had the same say as states with fewer people. Nothing was getting done, so America's leaders decided to try again.

Freedom for All

On May 25, 1787, twelve of the thirteen states sent delegates to Philadelphia to begin work on a new plan of government—the **Constitution**. As the Constitution was being written, there were all sorts of arguments, but after a two-year struggle, the United States had a wonderful plan that would stand the test of time.

In 1791 the **Bill of Rights** was added, which guaranteed Americans many freedoms, including the freedom to speak openly, to choose any religion, and to print whatever we want in the press.

There were 55 delegates present at the Constitutional Convention in 1787. George Washington (shown seated at his desk) was in charge of the meetings.

Words To Know

- **Equality**
  (ee-KWALL-a-tee)
  Treating all people exactly the same way.

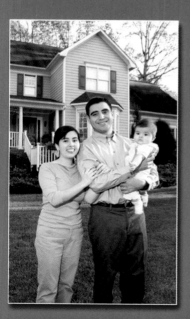

HAPPINESS comes when we know we can get decent jobs and put food on our tables. We can pursue happiness when we have time to do the things we love. Happiness comes from having opportunities!

At times in America's past, people from other lands and cultures were treated badly. **EQUALITY UNDER THE LAW** means that we must all be treated the same way.

LET'S REVIEW

Communities: The places we live

NOTICE

NO TRESPASSING ON THIS PROPERTY UNDER PENALTY OF LAW

Laws: Important rules written and carried out by government

STOP

Equality: Treating all people the same way

Three levels of government: local, state, and national

Basic American Principles

Life

SAVE OUR SCHOOL!

STOP

Liberty

The pursuit of happiness

Use pages 62-63 to complete questions 1-2.

1. Copy the graphic organizer and answer the question in each box.

What is government?		What is the basic job of government?

GOVERNMENT

Why do we need a government?

2. What are the three different levels of government of the United States?

Use pages 64-65 to answer questions 3-4.

3. The Declaration of Independence says that all people are born with three basic rights that cannot be taken away. What are they? What do they mean?

4. Another basic American principle is equality under the law. What does that mean?

5. What does the Bill of Rights guarantee all Americans?

IMAGINE IF...

• You are running for President of the United States. What is the most important promise you would make to the American people and why?

• The United States decided to change its form of government so that the leader of the country was a king or queen instead of an elected President. How do you think life would be different for you? For your parents? For your friends? For your children and grandkids in the future?

THINK AND DO

• Create an information pamphlet for someone who has just come to the United States that explains some of the basic principles held by Americans.

• Research and investigate where your local (community) government, state (Virginia) government, and national (United States) government are located.

• Think about the three basic rights stated in the Declaration of Independence. Choose the one you feel is the most important basic right and explain your choice.

CHAPTER 6

George Washington

Thomas Jefferson

Meet seven
people who
changed our
nation
forever.

Abraham Lincoln

AMERICAN HEROES

Thurgood Marshall

César Chávez

Martin Luther King, Jr.

The first capital of the United States was in New York City. George Washington is shown riding into the city to be sworn in as President of the United States on April 30, 1789. Two years later the capital moved to Philadelphia, Pennsylvania, before finally moving in 1800 to a new city built on the Potomac River—Washington, D.C.

GEORGE
WASHINGTON

- *He was the first President of the United States.*
- *He worked under the new republican form of government and helped put the basic principles into practice for the new nation.*

On the day George Washington became America's first President, he was scared. He had faced death on the battlefields of the Revolutionary War, but the thought of having to be the first person to run our brand-new nation terrified him.

Even though Washington did not want to be President, he knew his country needed him. He had been given a lot of power, but he swore not to use it for his own gain. He knew that he had to be unafraid to use his power if he needed to. He also knew he needed help. The first thing he did was form a "cabinet," which was not a piece of furniture, but a group of America's brightest men, to help him.

"First in War, First in Peace...

George Washington's **FIRST** loves were his home state and his farm at Mount Vernon. He was born in Virginia in 1732 and grew up to be a fine soldier and leader.

Washington became the **FIRST** commander-in-chief of America's Continental Army and led it to victory over the English.

Washington was the **FIRST** to sign the Constitution and the **FIRST** to be President under its rules. He appointed the **FIRST** Cabinet (which had four members), and also chose the **FIRST** Justices of the Supreme Court.

No More Kings

Many people wanted Washington to be made the king of the United States. Kings are not elected. They get the job from their parents or grab power using their armies. Kings rule for their entire lives and make all the rules by themselves. Washington believed that the President, and those who rule our country, should be *chosen* by America's citizens. The Constitutional Convention had set up the framework for this great experiment—**a republican form of government**.

Washington took office, and slowly the three branches of the new government began to do their jobs. A national bank was started so that we all had the same kind of money. As head of the armed forces, he defended the nation against threats from others.

Washington served as President for two terms—eight years. People begged him to stay on, but he wanted to return to the life he loved as a farmer. He died two years after he left office in 1799, at his home, Mt. Vernon, in Fairfax County, Virginia. His last words were "Tis well." America *was* well, thanks to one of our first heroes.

Today the Purple Heart is one of the highest honors a soldier can get. Washington created it to honor three of his bravest soldiers.

Words To Know
- **Republic**
(ree-PUB-lick)
A government in which the power is given to its citizens who choose people to represent them.

First in the Hearts of His Countrymen" -Henry "Light Horse Harry" Lee

At the request of our **FIRST** President, the nation's capital was moved to a spot near Washington's home. To honor him, it was named Washington.

Born 1732
Died 1799

"We should never despair. Our situation before has been unpromising and has changed for the better, so I trust, it will again."

THOMAS
JEFFERSON

- *He was born in Virginia.*
- *He was the third President of the United States.*
- *He wrote the Declaration of Independence, which states that people have certain rights.*
- *He was a leader who helped develop the country.*

Born 1743
Died 1826

"We hold these truths to be self-evident, that all men are created equal..."

It took many tries to write the Declaration. Jefferson was helped by Benjamin Franklin (at left) and John Adams (in the center)— two of America's greatest minds. Adams went on to become America's second President.

Thomas Jefferson was a tall, freckle-faced man with a secret fear. He hated speaking in public, but when it came to writing, he was a genius. The members of the Continental Congress, who gathered in Philadelphia in 1776, knew this. When they needed someone to draft a document that would cut America's ties with England, they turned to the 33-year-old representative from Virginia and asked him to write it.

The Power of the Pen

The **Declaration of Independence** changed the lives of millions of people. In it Jefferson wrote that all men were created equal, regardless of birth, wealth, or rank. He said that government was the servant, not the master, of the people. These were uncommon thoughts at a time when kings ruled and people bought and sold slaves.

Who *was* the man who wrote some of the most famous words in history? Thomas Jefferson was born in Virginia in 1743. He came from a wealthy family, and when his father died, he inherited more than 200 slaves. Owning slaves was common at the time. Jefferson wrote powerful words that said all men were equal even though he kept slaves all his life.

Freedom For All

After writing the Declaration, Jefferson returned home to make his words a reality in Virginia. He wrote the **Virginia Statute for Religious Freedom** in 1786. It later became the basis for the religion clause of the United States Constitution. Jefferson went on to do many great things, from serving as Governor of Virginia to being President of the United States from 1801-1809. During his presidency he doubled the size of the United States with the Louisiana Purchase—more than 800,000 square miles of land bought from France. He also sent Lewis and Clark on a very famous trip west to explore America's new lands.

His Proudest Moments

Jefferson's last great contribution was the founding of the **University of Virginia**. He did everything from finding the site to designing the buildings to planning what classes would be taught.

Thomas Jefferson—diplomat, architect, farmer, teacher, and inventor—died on July 4, 1826, exactly 50 years after his Declaration of Independence let freedom ring. We remember him as a great American who helped develop this country and change the course of history with the stroke of his pen.

"I Wish Most To Be Remembered…"

Even though Jefferson did many great things, there were three he cared about most.

He was most proud of:
1-The Declaration of Independence
2-The Virginia Statute for Religious Freedom
3- The creation of the University of Virginia, which became one of the world's best universities

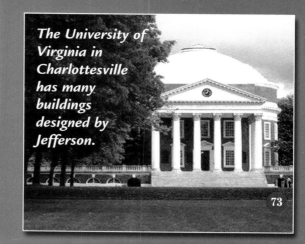

The University of Virginia in Charlottesville has many buildings designed by Jefferson.

From a Log Cabin to the White House

Lincoln was born in Kentucky in 1809. He came from a poor family but believed that hard work and education would help him do well in life.

Lincoln had lots of jobs. He split fence rails, worked in a store, and drove a river boat. He was a soldier, a lawyer, and a judge. He ran for office and finally became our 16th President.

Five days after the Civil War ended, John Wilkes Booth shot and killed President Lincoln as he watched a play in Washington, D.C.

ABRAHAM LINCOLN

- *He was the United States President when the country was divided over the issue of equality for all people.*

- *He helped free enslaved African Americans.*

The United States was born with a promise: life, liberty, and the pursuit of happiness. But there were millions of people living in America in the 1850s who had *terrible* lives, *no* liberty, and *no* hope of ever pursuing happiness. These were the enslaved African Americans who toiled in the fields of the Southern states. The life of a slave was filled with back-breaking work with no rewards and no hope of freedom, ever.

Abraham Lincoln knew slavery—the buying, selling, and owning of human beings—was wrong. When he ran for President in 1860, he vowed to stop the spread of slavery into the new states that were becoming part of our nation.

A New President, A Horrible War

When Lincoln won the election, many Southern states—where slavery had long been a way of life—decided to break away and start their own new country. On February 9, 1861, the Confederate States of America was formed, and the Civil War began. Like a family torn apart by a divorce, our nation was ripped in two.

North Against South, Brother Against Brother

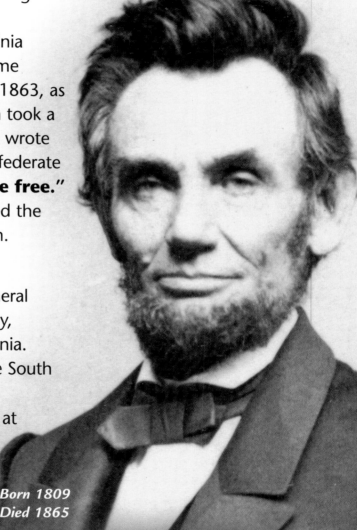

This painting shows the horror of war on a Virginia battlefield.

Virginia left the Union—another name for the United States—on April 17, 1861, and joined the eleven-state Confederacy (con-FED-er-a-see). Virginia itself was torn apart when its western counties chose to break away and rejoin the Union, forming a new state called West Virginia.

Year after year the war dragged on. The Virginia farmlands of Bull Run and Fredericksburg became battlegrounds, then graveyards. On January 1, 1863, as the nation reached its third year at war, Lincoln took a bold step. In his Emancipation Proclamation he wrote that **"all persons held as slaves"** in the Confederate states (but not elsewhere) **"are, and...shall be free."** By war's end, almost 200,000 freed slaves joined the Union Army to help the North defeat the South.

Free at Last

The Civil War ended on April 9, 1865, as General Robert E. Lee, commander of the Southern Army, surrendered at Appomattox Courthouse in Virginia. Millions had died or been crippled. Much of the South was in ruins.

Five days later, as Lincoln enjoyed an evening at Ford's Theater in Washington, D.C., John Wilkes Booth, an angry Southerner, shot the President. Lincoln died the next day.

Today we honor Abraham Lincoln as one of America's greatest Presidents. He believed that we live in a land where *all* people, regardless of the color of their skin, deserve the same chances for life, liberty, and the pursuit of happiness.

Born 1809
Died 1865

"As I would not be a slave, so I would not be a master. This expresses my idea of democracy."

ROSA
PARKS

- *She was an African American woman who refused to give up her seat on a public bus even though it was the law where she lived.*
- *She helped to bring about changes in laws and worked so that all people would have equal rights.*

Superheroes do not have to have big muscles or wear capes. Sometimes very ordinary people can perform super acts. Rosa Parks, a seamstress in Montgomery, Alabama, was a true superhero. She helped to change a law that no one thought could be changed, and she did it by doing one very little but very brave thing.

For months she and her friends had been planning it—waiting for the right moment to make their move. That day came on December 1, 1955.

Words To Know

- **Boycott**
  (BOY-cot)
  To refuse to do business with a person, company, or nation in order to punish or show disapproval.

- **Segregation**
  (seg-re-GAY-shun)
  The act or practice of keeping people or groups apart, which leads to inequality

Born 1913
Died 2005

"I do the very best I can to look upon life with optimism and hope ..."

A World Apart

Rosa Parks was born in 1913 in Alabama, a state with strict **segregation** laws. African Americans had to go to separate schools and play in separate parks. They had to give up their seats to white people on trains or buses. It was a time when most African Americans could not vote, and a person of color could be killed just "because."

Mrs. Parks went to college, got married, and got one of the only jobs she could—sewing. She and her husband Raymond joined the NAACP—*The National Association for the Advancement of Colored People*—a group devoted to making life better for African Americans.

The Mother of Civil Rights

On a chilly December evening, Mrs. Parks got on the bus to go home and took a seat in a section reserved for white people. When the driver told her to give up her seat to a white man, she quietly said, "No." She was arrested and put in jail!

Leaders of the black community, including a young pastor, Dr. Martin Luther King, Jr., called for a **boycott** of the bus company. That boycott lasted 382 days. The city's African Americans walked miles or carpooled to get to their destinations. The bus company almost went out of business.

In November of 1956, the U.S. Supreme Court struck down the segregation laws on public transportation. Blacks and whites would now be treated the same when they rode on buses or trains, but the long struggle for civil rights was far from over. Rosa Parks kept on playing a big part in that struggle, always ready to fight for people who were treated badly simply because of the color of their skin.

One Small Step...

Until 1955 African Americans could only sit at the back of the bus. They had to give up their seats to white people.

Mrs. Parks would not get up! She was arrested, finger-printed, and sent to jail.

More than 42,000 African Americans started walking instead of riding. They stopped using the buses for more than a year until the laws changed.

Thurgood Marshall was the grandson of former slaves. He studied hard, went to college, and became a great lawyer.

His most famous court case was called *Brown vs. the Board of Education of Topeka*. Because of that victory, Ruby Bridges became the first black child to go to a white school. Grown-ups had to protect her in the beginning, and she became a national symbol.

In 1967 Marshall was chosen to be a U.S. Supreme Court judge. He was the first person of color to wear the robes of a high court justice—a very great honor.

THURGOOD MARSHALL

- He was a lawyer who defended people at a time when not all people had equal rights.
- He was the first African-American Justice of the United States Supreme Court.

"Separate but equal." That was the law in the early 1900s (and before), but people were not *really* treated equally back then. White children went to whites-only schools. African American children went to schools with other children of color. Their schools were not as good as the schools the white children attended.

Unfair!

Thurgood Marshall was the man who helped change that. He was born in Baltimore, Maryland, in 1908. He was turned away from the Law School at the University of Maryland because he was not white. He *knew* he had to change America's unfair laws.

Ruby Bridges and the famous painting she inspired

Thurgood Marshall became a lawyer for the NAACP, the *National Association for the Advancement of Colored People.* **Desegregation** and equality were his goals, and he spent his life working for them.

Upholding the Constitution

Marshall made it his life's work to get equal rights for African Americans in housing, voting, and especially education. His most famous victory came in 1954 with **Brown vs. the Board of Education of Topeka**, the case that let black and white children go to the same schools together. He believed in the wisdom of the Constitution with all his heart and used it to support his actions.

He became a judge in New York in 1961 and six years later was chosen by President Lyndon Johnson to be a U.S. Supreme Court Justice. That is the highest honor a judge can be given. For the next 24 years he worked to give *every* American citizen equal protection under the Constitution that he so cherished.

Thurgood Marshall has been honored with statues, scholarships, and even a postage stamp.

Thurgood Marshall

Words To Know

- **Desegregation**
  (dee-seg-ra-GAY-shun) The mixing of racial or religious groups together into a community after they have been kept apart.

Do you recognize this building? It is the Supreme Court, where Thurgood Marshall had just won his biggest case. Little did he know, he would return here to become a famous judge.

*Born 1908
Died 1993*

"**Equal means getting the same thing, at the same time and in the same place.**"

79

MARTIN LUTHER
KING, JR.

- *He was an African-American minister who worked for equal rights for all people.*
- *He helped bring about changes in laws through peaceful means.*

Born 1929
Died 1968

How much would you be willing to put up with to change something you *knew* was wrong? Could you stand to be screamed at or thrown in jail? Would you give up if someone bombed your house?

Martin Luther King, Jr. was arrested almost 20 times. He was beaten and got many death threats, but he never behaved in an angry way, and he never gave up fighting for the rights of his fellow human beings.

"I have a dream that my four little children will one day live in a nation where they will not be judged by the color of their skin but by the content of their character."

Martin Luther King, Jr. was born in 1929 in Georgia. His father, grandfather, and great-grandfather were all preachers. He followed in their path.

At the age of 19, he became a minister in Alabama. African Americans were being treated badly in much of the South. He was arrested many times.

Dr. King formed the Southern Christian Leadership Conference in 1957 to fight segregation. One year later the U.S. Congress passed the first Civil Rights Act since the end of the Civil War.

SOUTHERN CHRISTIAN LEADERSHIP CONFERENCE

WE SHALL OVERCOME

Between 1957 and 1968, Dr. King traveled over six million miles. He gave over 2,500 speeches. He led a huge boycott in Alabama after Rosa Parks was arrested for refusing to give her bus seat to a white man. He spoke to more than 250,000 people at a peaceful march on Washington, D.C., and he dared them to dream of a land where people were judged by their hearts, not their skin. He urged people to use peaceful means to change things and taught them about **civil disobedience** as a way to make those changes. His powerful voice was heard by millions, and several unfair laws were struck down because of what he said.

The Promised Land

On the evening of April 4, 1968, Dr. King was shot in Memphis, Tennessee. Sadly, he died soon after at the age of 39. Dr. King peacefully worked for change. He did not speak in anger. He did not hit back. His life is proof that dignity, patience, and faith can move mountains.

Words To Know

- **Civil disobedience**
  (DIS-oh-BEE-dee-ens)

Refusing to obey laws that are unfair; using non-violent public protests, such as a group of people blocking the entrance to a building.

Soon after his "I Have a Dream" speech on the steps of the Lincoln Memorial in 1963, the U.S. Constitution was changed so that African Americans would no longer be unfairly kept from voting.

In 1964 Dr. King won the Nobel Peace Prize. He was the youngest man ever to win it. He gave all his prize money to the civil rights movement.

When Dr. King was killed in 1968, people were sad. Many got very angry, and there were riots in some cities. Today we remember Dr. King as a man of peace who died trying to make the world a better place.

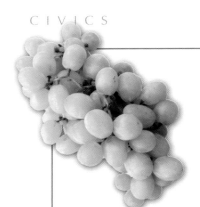

CÉSAR
Chávez

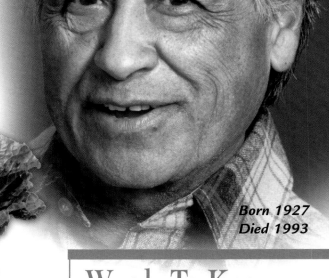

Born 1927
Died 1993

- *He was a Mexican American who worked to improve conditions for farm workers.*

Lettuce and grapes are two foods that many of us eat, but how would you feel if you knew people were suffering and even dying as they worked to get these foods onto your table? César Chávez knew all about the terrible working conditions of the migrant workers. In the 1960s he used lettuce and grapes as symbols of the horrors farm workers faced as they labored to feed our nation.

Homeless and Hopeless

César Chávez was born on a small family farm in Arizona on March 31, 1927. Ten years later he found himself homeless and hungry when his family could not pay their rent during the Great Depression—a time when many businesses closed and there were few jobs.

To survive, the Chávez family became **migrant** workers. The only jobs they could get were picking fruit and vegetables. In time, his family ended up in California, which had many farms. They moved every few weeks as each crop came in. Going to school was difficult since migrant families moved so often. By eighth grade Chávez was forced to quit school. He decided to join the U.S. Navy, then after serving his country, came home to begin a life of back-breaking work and terrible living conditions.

Words To Know

- **Migrant**
(MY-grint)
A person who moves from place to place seeking work.

- **Union**
(YOU-nyun)
A group of people who work to improve conditions and wages at a company.

A migrant worker in front of his family's home.

> ## "We are suffering. We have suffered. And we are not afraid to suffer in order to win our cause."

Si Se Puede—It Can Be Done

César Chávez saw the awful working and living conditions of his fellow workers and knew he had to do something. In 1962 Chávez started the *National Farm Workers Association*, a **union** that became the *United Farm Workers of America*. To get decent wages, housing, and medical care for farm workers, he began to lead union members in strikes. Workers stopped picking and left the crops to rot. Then Chávez asked shoppers to boycott crops grown by farms that did not pay decent wages. Sales of grapes and lettuce fell, and the growers finally gave in.

There was another problem. Poisons were used to kill insects on the crops—poisons that were also killing farm workers, so Chávez went on hunger strikes to call attention to the problem. In 1988 Chávez did not eat for 36 days to protest the use of poisons. He became world-famous for his courage.

A Life of Dignity

In a country that measures success in the amount of money a person earns, Chávez might be thought of as a failure. He never owned a house and did not go to college, but he left behind a mighty legacy—the idea that everyone is entitled to a decent life. He said, "Our struggle is not easy. Those who oppose our cause are rich and powerful and they have many allies in high places. We are poor. Our allies are few. But we have something the rich do not own. We have our bodies and spirits and the justice of our cause as our weapons."

A Life of Service

Chávez grew up in Arizona. He was very poor. He had to quit school and go to work to help support his family.

Chávez began to work with the Community Service Organization, a group that helped Mexican Americans. He led strikes and started grape and lettuce boycotts. People stopped buying these crops.

With crops going unpicked or unsold, farm owners had to improve working conditions.

After he died Chávez's memory was honored with a stamp and the Presidential Medal of Freedom—two great honors.

USA 37 CESAR E. CHAVEZ 2003

LET'S REVIEW

SEVEN IMPORTANT AMERICANS TO REMEMBER

 **George Washington:** America's first President

Thomas Jefferson: Wrote the Declaration of Independence

Abraham Lincoln: Helped free enslaved African Americans

 **Rosa Parks:** Refused to give up her seat on a bus which helped change bad laws

Thurgood Marshall: First African-American Supreme Court justice

Martin Luther King, Jr.: Helped change the laws through peaceful means

César Chávez: A Mexican American who fought to help farm workers

Use the page numbers below to complete the chart on a separate sheet of paper.

Famous American	Who was he or she?	How did he or she work to defend basic American principles?
George Washington *(pages 70-71)*		
Thomas Jefferson *(pages 72-73)*		
Abraham Lincoln *(pages 74-75)*		
Rosa Parks *(pages 76-77)*		
Thurgood Marshall *(pages 78-79)*		
Martin Luther King, Jr. *(pages 80-81)*		
César Chávez *(pages 82-83)*		

THINK AND DO

• Pick one person from this chapter whom you admire the most. Write a letter to that person explaining how his or her contribution helped change America and why you admire that person's courage.

• Review the three Presidents from the chapter and brainstorm a list of all the different things George Washington, Thomas Jefferson, and Abraham Lincoln did (architect, farmer, shopkeeper, etc.). Select at least six items from the list to create a presidential mobile by drawing pictures and writing.

IMAGINE IF...

• You have the opportunity to travel back in time to visit one of the seven American heroes studied in this chapter. Which one would you chose? Describe how different America was back then compared to the way it is today.

• What if Abraham Lincoln did not free the enslaved African Americans in the United States? How do you think the lives of Rosa Parks, Thurgood Marshall, and Martin Luther King, Jr. would be different?

REVIEW QUESTIONS

WHAT MAKES AMERICA SPECIAL?

From holidays to great traditions,
discover the wonderful things that unite
us as Americans.

Fourth of July fireworks burst over the Statue of Liberty—a symbol of freedom all over the world.

Words To Know

- **Veteran**

   (VET-ur-in)

   A person who has served in the military, which includes the Army, Navy, Air Force, Marines, Coast Guard, and National Guard.

There are over 200,000 soldiers and sailors—from every war America has fought—buried at Arlington National Cemetery in Virginia.

ALL-AMERICAN HOLIDAYS

• *America has set aside special days to honor people who have served to protect our country's freedom.*

Everyone loves a parade, and it is fun to get a day off from school on a holiday, but there is a very important reason we are celebrating. Many of our special celebrations are reminders of people who did brave and amazing things to help make America great.

Heroes Forever

We celebrate Presidents' Day in February to salute George Washington and Abraham Lincoln. We remember Martin Luther King, Jr. in January. On the 4th of July, we proudly cheer our nation's fight for independence.

But there are two holidays that are especially important. They do not honor famous men. Instead they celebrate the bravery and courage of ordinary people just like you—the **veterans** who have served our country.

Celebrating Bravery

Memorial Day was first called *Decoration Day* because people "decorated" the graves of soldiers who had died in the Civil War. Beginning in May of 1868, family and friends started placing flowers and flags at the graves of the war's dead. Sadly, the Civil War was not America's only war. Memorial Day became **a day to honor all the men and women who had died fighting for freedom**. In 1971 Congress made Memorial Day a national holiday to be celebrated on the last Monday in May.

Every November 11 we celebrate **Veterans Day—a day to honor everyone who has served in the military**. November 11, 1918, was the day World War I ended—the last day of one of the bloodiest wars of all time. To welcome the return of peace to the world, a day was set aside to salute *all* the soldiers who had given up so much.

So this year on Memorial Day and Veterans Day, enjoy the picnics and parades, but stop and think about the people who gave their all for freedom.

Two Very Special Holidays to Remember

MEMORIAL DAY is always held on the last Monday in May to honor all those who died fighting for America. This girl has just placed a small flag at the Vietnam Memorial in Washington, D.C., which lists the names of all those who lost their lives in the Vietnam War.

VETERANS DAY falls in November. It is a day of recognition and respect for *all* Americans who served in the military. This man is a proud veteran of World War II—one of the biggest wars ever.

89

You Can Be a Hero!

Kids your age are making a big difference in the world. They do it by pitching in and helping in their communities.

Some kids serve meals at soup kitchens.

Many kids help protect the Earth's special resources.

Some make good neighbors by helping with town clean-ups.

HOMETOWN
HEROES

- *There are many ways that people can serve their community, state, and nation.*

You do not have to be a famous person to make the world a better place. You can pitch in right now! Here are some of the ways people can serve their community, state, and nation.

Let's Volunteer

Many towns depend on teams of volunteers to run fire departments and ambulance services. These brave men and women rush out, sometimes in the middle of the night, to help their neighbors in the event of an emergency.

These volunteer firefighters are fighting a big blaze. They do not get paid for their service and sometimes have to leap out of bed in the middle of the night or leave a family dinner to save a life.

This man serves in the U.S. Navy. He is away at sea many months of the year, far from his family.

Pitching In Around Virginia

Picking up litter, helping to bring meals to elderly neighbors, and coaching soccer or baseball are just some of the ways people help out in their communities. Cities and counties need people to help run them, so interested citizens can run for mayor, sit on a town council, or be a part of the school board. Some Virginians serve their state by helping people vote on election day.

Serving with Pride

Many brave men and women sign up to serve their country as soldiers and sailors, spending time in America's Armed Forces. Some join the Peace Corps, Teach for America, or other groups that send people to places that need help.

There is one last and very important way we can serve our towns and country and that is by voting. All citizens age 18 or older should vote. It is one of the greatest rights we have as Americans—a chance to speak out and make our voices heard and to help determine the course of our nation's future.

AMERICA, THE DIVERSE

• The American people come from diverse ethnic and national origins and are united as Americans by basic American principles.

In the early 1900s a great wave of people left Europe for America, hoping for a better life. They carried everything they owned in cardboard suitcases, trunks, and sacks. They were tired and scared when they arrived—not sure what life would be like in the United States.

Coming Together

Many thousands of years ago people rarely left home. They never saw people who looked different from themselves. The Africans were the first people to leave their homelands a million years ago—fanning out to populate the world. Ancient Egyptians and Greeks were some of the first to write stories of what they saw on their journeys. **Diversity** was a big surprise at first. Their explorers brought back diaries from their voyages, along with wild (and often *very* confused) descriptions of the people, places, and things they had seen.

First Contacts

As people began to travel from continent to continent, Asians saw Africans for the first time. Europeans saw Asians.

Something interesting happened in America. It became the first place on Earth where many people of different colors and **ethnic origins** had to live side by side. The United States became the first place where Native Americans, Africans, Europeans, and Asians all *had* to learn to work together. America became the world's first truly diverse nation—a place where we learned to appreciate other people's **customs**.

We have worked hard to make this a land where everyone is treated the same. It has not always been easy, and we have made a lot of mistakes. We still have a lot to learn, but America will always be a land of promise.

Words To Know

- **Diversity**
(Di-VER-sit-ee)
The differences between people such as age, religion, and race.

- **Ethnic Origin**
People who share a common race, birthplace, religion, language, or culture.

- **Customs**
(CUST-umz)
Ways of doing things that are passed from one generation to the next.

In the United States, children from many different places came face to face with boys and girls who looked, spoke, and dressed differently.

These children's families come from six different continents!

WHY DIVERSITY IS COOL

- *Without diversity we might not have the things that make life so much fun.*

Clothing: Who Wears the Pants?

American Indians wore long deerskin leggings. The new settlers from Europe found them to be more comfortable than their own baggy breeches. In the mid-1800s a German immigrant named Levi Strauss made pants for gold miners out of denim. He used brass rivets to make the pockets extra strong. Blue jeans were born!

Even our shoes tell a tale of diversity, from Indian mocassins, to European wood-soled clogs, to Greek and Roman style sandals.

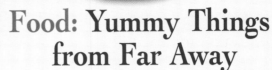

Food: Yummy Things from Far Away

When people moved to America, they brought their favorite foods with them. Once they were here, other folks tasted these new foods and loved them!

- Enslaved Africans used ground **peanuts** in many of their dishes.
- **Pizza** is the Italian word for "pie." Flat breads with toppings were popular even in ancient Rome!
- **Donuts and cookies** came here with Dutch settlers.
- **Hamburgers** and **frankfurters** are named for German towns—Hamburg and Frankfurt. **Pretzels** came from Germany but got their start in Italy.
- **Chocolate** came from South America. Spanish explorers brought it back to Europe and sweetened it.
- **Tacos** and **tortillas** came from Mexico. Corn was sacred to many American Indians.
- **Ice cream** may have been first made in China.
- **Coffee** came from Africa.

Music:
Red, White, and the Blues

Turn on a radio or MP3 player and you will be listening to diversity in action. Today's hippest tunes have grown out of the music of many lands, especially Africa. From jazz, to the blues, to gospel, to rock, to rap, to hip-hop, our most popular music grooves to an African beat.

Enslaved Africans beat out rhythms with their hands and feet because drums were not allowed. Music was a way to forget the sadness of slavery and to pray. More importantly, it was a way to "talk" secretly to other slaves and arrange meetings without the master knowing.

From Jazz to Rock to Rap

The enslaved Africans had "call and answer" music and melodies made up on-the-go instead of playing exact notes. That grew into jazz—a type of music full of emotion. Rock 'n' roll came along and was also inspired by the drum beats and strummed strings of African music mixed with European melodies. Rap and hip-hop have roots that go even farther back—to the storytellers of West Africa.

Spicy Salsa

Salsa is a tangy dip for chips, but it is also a hot and spicy style of music and dance—a mix of African and Spanish rhythms—and it is great fun. These days music is a world-wide blend of sounds. Rappers sing to 200-year-old European melodies. Music truly rocks!

Louis Armstrong was one of America's greatest musicians. He learned to play the horn in reform school, a type of school for kids who get in trouble with the law. He played jazz—a kind of music where the melody changed at the whim of the musician. Jazz soon was being played all over the world.

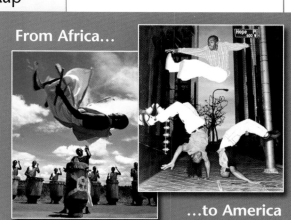

From Africa...

...to America

Break dancing and hip-hop are borrowed from African traditions, but they also mix in Asian Kung Fu moves, the Brazilian fighting art of Capoeira (ka-PWE-rah), Latin dancing styles, and much more!

Americans love to dance! Square dancing is a combination of clog dancing, reels, and polkas from Europe.

The Right to Vote

African Americans and women were not always treated as equals. They could not vote! The U.S. Constitution had to be changed to include them. That took years and years.

In 1867 African Americans finally became citizens of the United States. In 1870 they got the right to vote, but many were still turned away from the polls by unfair taxes or odd "rules," such as being able to recite certain laws perfectly. In 1964 a law was passed that truly gave *all* African Americans the right to vote.

Women finally got their first chance to vote for President in 1920 after the U. S. Constitution was amended to include women.

WE ARE ALL
EQUAL

- *We are all united as Americans by basic American principles.*

You now know that Americans are united by something very special—the right to life, liberty, the pursuit of happiness, and equality under the law. These are rights than cannot be taken away.

We must all have the same chances to learn, get jobs, and have a safe place to live, no matter where we come from. We must all have a voice in the way our country is run.

Vote for Me!

You also now know that the United States has a **republican form of government**. We choose people to be the President, a governor, a senator, or a mayor because they have promised to do things the way we would like.

In our **representative democracy** every American citizen 18 or older can vote for the people who make our laws. They do this by voting in elections. Every year on the first Tuesday of November, voters go to the polls—a place to vote—and select their favorite candidates and decide on important issues facing the nation and our state.

One Promise, One Dream

Our nation was born with a promise of freedom. That freedom comes from having a say in how we live. In the past we were sometimes afraid of people who moved to the United States from other lands, so we wrote laws to keep them out. Our leaders thought these newcomers might try to overthrow our government, but we have learned that people from different backgrounds can help make our nation stronger and better!

Our American Dream

Americans have always been dreamers, from this land's first peoples, to the early settlers, to the African Americans yearning for freedom, to our newest immigrants. We dream of a country where people of every color and every land can live peacefully. We must always remember that we are *all* Americans and we are *all* created equal. We are united by a hunger for freedom and a thirst for justice. Together we can help make America's dreams come true.

"I pledge allegiance to the flag," are words that unite us all as Americans and remind us of our nation's promise.

Words To Know

- **Republican form of government**

A representative democracy where we elect people to speak for us in the making of laws.

PROUD TO BE A
VIRGINIA DEMOCRAT

VOTE REPUBLICAN

Today America has two main political parties— the Republicans and the Democrats. Each has different ideas about how America should be run. Every year across the country, candidates from each party run against each other in elections.

LET'S REVIEW

MAJOR HOLIDAYS

Veterans Day

Memorial Day

BASIC PRINCIPLES

Republic

Republican Form of Government

WAYS TO SERVE

Being a volunteer

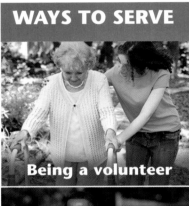
Serving in the government

Joining the military

Community projects

Voting

DIVERSITY

Diverse foods

Diverse clothing

Diverse music

REVIEW QUESTIONS

Use pages 88-89 to answer questions 1 and 2.
1. Whom do we honor on Veterans Day, and when is it observed?
2. Whom do we honor on Memorial Day, and when is it observed?

Use pages 90-91 to answer question 3.
3. List at least three ways people can serve their community, state, and nation.

Use pages 94-95 to answer question 4.
4. There are many benefits to having diversity in America. For each of the benefits listed below, give one example of something that has now become part of our American heritage.
  - Clothing
  - Food
  - Music

Use pages 96-97 to answer questions 5-6.
5. What basic American principles unite the people of the United States?
6. The United States government is a representative democracy. What does that mean?

THINK AND DO

- Americans come from different ethnic origins and different countries. Talk to your family and ask them from which country or countries their ancestors came. Find the country on a map of the world and use the map legend to determine how many miles your ancestors traveled to get to America.

- People of all ages can volunteer to serve their community, state, and nation. In what volunteer activity would you most like to serve and why?

IMAGINE IF...

- You have been asked to create a new national holiday. What holiday would you invent and why? When and how would this holiday be celebrated?

- There is a new student in your class from another country. What do you think are the most important American traditions the student should learn? How would you help that person learn these traditions?

FUN VIRGINIA FACTS

State Bird
Cardinal

State Tree and
Flower
Dogwood

State Dog
**American Fox
Hound**

State Boat
**The Chesapeake
Bay Deadrise**

State Fish
Brook Trout

State Dance
The Square Dance

State Insect
**Swallowtail
Butterfly**

State Drink
Milk

- 10th state to join the Union (June 25, 1788)
- 12th most populous state

- 37th largest state
- Highest point–Mt. Rogers
- Largest city–Virginia Beach

- Hottest day–July 5, 1954 (110° F) • Coldest Day– Feb. 10, 1899 (-29° F)

PICTURE CREDITS

DOCUMENTS AND MAPS

Reference materials
for additional learning.

IN CONGRESS, JULY 4, 1776.

The unanimous Declaration of the thirteen united States of America,

When in the Course of human events, it becomes necessary for one people to dissolve the political bands which have connected them with another, and to assume among the powers of the earth, the separate and equal station to which the Laws of Nature and of Nature's God entitle them, a decent respect to the opinions of mankind requires that they should declare the causes which impel them to the separation.

We hold these truths to be self-evident, that all men are created equal, that they are endowed by their Creator with certain unalienable Rights, that among these are Life, Liberty and the pursuit of Happiness.—That to secure these rights, Governments are instituted among Men, deriving their just powers from the consent of the governed,—That whenever any Form of Government becomes destructive of these ends, it is the Right of the People to alter or to abolish it, and to institute new Government, laying its foundation on such principles and organizing its powers in such form, as to them shall seem most likely to effect their Safety and Happiness. Prudence, indeed, will dictate that Governments long established should not be changed for light and transient causes; and accordingly all experience hath shewn, that mankind are more disposed to suffer, while evils are sufferable, than to right themselves by abolishing the forms to which they are accustomed. But when a long train of abuses and usurpations, pursuing invariably the same Object evinces a design to reduce them under absolute Despotism, it is their right, it is their duty, to throw off such Government, and to provide new Guards for their future security.—Such has been the patient sufferance of these Colonies; and such is now the necessity which constrains them to alter their former Systems of Government. The history of the present King of Great Britain is a history of repeated injuries and usurpations, all having in direct object the establishment of an absolute Tyranny over these States. To prove this, let Facts be submitted to a candid world.

He has refused his Assent to Laws, the most wholesome and necessary for the public good.—He has forbidden his Governors to pass Laws of immediate and pressing importance, unless suspended in their operation till his Assent should be obtained; and when so suspended, he has utterly neglected to attend to them.—He has refused to pass other Laws for the accommodation of large districts of people, unless those people would relinquish the right of Representation in the Legislature, a right inestimable to them and formidable to tyrants only.—He has called together legislative bodies at places unusual, uncomfortable, and distant from the depository of their Public Records, for the sole purpose of fatiguing them into compliance with his measures.—He has dissolved Representative Houses repeatedly, for opposing with manly firmness his invasions on the rights of the people.—He has refused for a long time, after such dissolutions, to cause others to be elected; whereby the Legislative powers, incapable of Annihilation, have returned to the People at large for their exercise; the State remaining in the mean time exposed to all the dangers of invasion from without, and convulsions within.—He has endeavoured to prevent the population of these States; for that purpose obstructing the Laws for Naturalization of Foreigners; refusing to pass others to encourage their migrations hither, and raising the conditions of new Appropriations of Lands.—He has obstructed the Administration of Justice, by refusing his Assent to Laws for establishing Judiciary powers.—He has made Judges dependent on his Will alone, for the tenure of their offices, and the amount and payment of their salaries.—He has erected a multitude of New Offices, and sent hither swarms of Officers to harrass our people, and eat out their substance.—He has kept among us, in times of peace, Standing Armies without the Consent of our legislatures.—He has affected to render the Military independent of and superior to the Civil power.—He has combined with others to subject us to a jurisdiction foreign to our constitution, and unacknowledged by our laws; giving his Assent to their Acts of pretended Legislation:—For Quartering large bodies of armed troops among us:—For protecting them, by a mock Trial, from punishment for any Murders which they should commit on the Inhabitants of these States:—For cutting off our Trade with all parts of the world:—For imposing Taxes on us without our Consent:—For depriving us in many cases, of the benefits of Trial by Jury:—For transporting us beyond Seas to be tried for pretended offences:—For abolishing the free System of English Laws in a neighbouring Province, establishing therein an Arbitrary government, and enlarging its Boundaries so as to render it at once an example and fit instrument for introducing the same absolute rule into these Colonies:—For taking away our Charters, abolishing our most valuable Laws, and altering fundamentally the Forms of our Governments:—For suspending our own Legislatures, and declaring themselves invested with power to legislate for us in all cases whatsoever.—He has abdicated Government here, by declaring us out of his Protection and waging War against us.—He has plundered our seas, ravaged our Coasts, burnt our towns, and destroyed the lives of our people.—He is at this time transporting large Armies of foreign Mercenaries to compleat the works of death, desolation and tyranny, already begun with circumstances of Cruelty & perfidy scarcely paralleled in the most barbarous ages, and totally unworthy the Head of a civilized nation.—He has constrained our fellow Citizens taken Captive on the high Seas to bear Arms against their country, to become the executioners of their friends and Brethren, or to fall themselves by their Hands.—He has excited domestic insurrections amongst us, and has endeavoured to bring on the inhabitants of our frontiers, the merciless Indian Savages, whose known rule of warfare, is an undistinguished destruction of all ages, sexes and conditions. In every stage of these Oppressions We have Petitioned for Redress in the most humble terms: Our repeated Petitions have been answered only by repeated injury. A Prince, whose character is thus marked by every act which may define a Tyrant, is unfit to be the ruler of a free people.

Nor have We been wanting in attentions to our British brethren. We have warned them from time to time of attempts by their legislature to extend an unwarrantable jurisdiction over us. We have reminded them of the circumstances of our emigration and settlement here. We have appealed to their native justice and magnanimity, and we have conjured them by the ties of our common kindred to disavow these usurpations, which, would inevitably interrupt our connections and correspondence. They too have been deaf to the voice of justice and of consanguinity. We must, therefore, acquiesce in the necessity, which denounces our Separation, and hold them, as we hold the rest of mankind, Enemies in War, in Peace Friends.

We, therefore, the Representatives of the united States of America, in General Congress, Assembled, appealing to the Supreme Judge of the world for the rectitude of our intentions, do, in the Name, and by Authority of the good People of these Colonies, solemnly publish and declare, That these United Colonies are, and of Right ought to be Free and Independent States; that they are Absolved from all Allegiance to the British Crown, and that all political connection between them and the State of Great Britain, is and ought to be totally dissolved; and that as Free and Independent States, they have full Power to levy War, conclude Peace, contract Alliances, establish Commerce, and to do all other Acts and Things which Independent States may of right do.—And for the support of this Declaration, with a firm reliance on the Protection of Divine Providence, we mutually pledge to each other our Lives, our Fortunes and our sacred Honor.

John Hancock

Button Gwinnett
Lyman Hall
Geo Walton.

Wm Hooper
Joseph Hewes,
John Penn

Edward Rutledge.

Thos Heyward Junr.
Thomas Lynch Junr.
Arthur Middleton

Samuel Chase
Wm Paca
Thos Stone
Charles Carroll of Carrollton

George Wythe
Richard Henry Lee
Th Jefferson
Benj Harrison
Thos Nelson jr.
Francis Lightfoot Lee
Carter Braxton

Robt Morris
Benjamin Rush
Benj. Franklin
John Morton
Geo Clymer
Jas. Smith
Geo. Taylor
James Wilson
Geo. Ross
Caesar Rodney
Geo Read
Tho M:Kean

Wm Floyd
Phil. Livingston
Frans. Lewis
Lewis Morris

Richd Stockton
Jno Witherspoon
Fras Hopkinson
John Hart
Abra Clark

Josiah Bartlett
Wm Whipple
Saml Adams
John Adams
Robt Treat Paine
Elbridge Gerry
Step Hopkins
William Ellery
Roger Sherman
Sam el Huntington
Wm Williams
Oliver Wolcott
Matthew Thornton

DECLARATION OF INDEPENDENCE

Written by Thomas Jefferson and signed on July 4, 1776

Thomas Jefferson

WHAT WAS IT?

This document ended our belonging to England. It marked the birth of the United States of America.

A FAMOUS PART

"We hold these truths to be self-evident, that all men are created equal, that they are endowed by their Creator with certain unalienable Rights, that among these are Life, Liberty and the pursuit of Happiness."

WHAT JEFFERSON SAID

1. We are born with rights that no one can take away from us.
2. If a government does something that hurts us, we have the right to change things.
3. England's king has taken away our rights and will not listen to us. He has made things very hard for us.
4. We have tried to tell the King our problems, but he will not listen.
5. We have no choice but to break away from England and govern ourselves.

WHAT HAPPENED?

We became the United States of America and went to war to break free of English rule. Brave George Washington led us to victory and went on to become our first, and one of our greatest, U.S. Presidents.

We the People

of the United States, in Order to form a more perfect Union, establish Justice, insure domestic Tranquility, provide for the common defence, promote the general Welfare, and secure the Blessings of Liberty to ourselves and our Posterity, do ordain and establish this Constitution for the United States of America.

Article. 1.

Section. 1. All legislative Powers herein granted shall be vested in a Congress of the United States, which shall consist of a Senate and House of Representatives.

Section. 2. The House of Representatives shall be composed of Members chosen every second Year by the People of the several States, and the Electors in each State shall have the Qualifications requisite for Electors of the most numerous Branch of the State Legislature.

No Person shall be a Representative who shall not have attained to the Age of twenty five Years, and been seven Years a Citizen of the United States, and who shall not, when elected, be an Inhabitant of that State in which he shall be chosen.

Representatives and direct Taxes shall be apportioned among the several States which may be included within this Union, according to their respective Numbers, which shall be determined by adding to the whole Number of free Persons, including those bound to Service for a Term of Years, and excluding Indians not taxed, three fifths of all other Persons. The actual Enumeration shall be made within three Years after the first Meeting of the Congress of the United States, and within every subsequent Term of ten Years, in such Manner as they shall by Law direct. The Number of Representatives shall not exceed one for every thirty Thousand, but each State shall have at Least one Representative; and until such enumeration shall be made, the State of New Hampshire shall be entitled to chuse three, Massachusetts eight, Rhode Island and Providence Plantations one, Connecticut five, New York six, New Jersey four, Pennsylvania eight, Delaware one, Maryland six, Virginia ten, North Carolina five, South Carolina five, and Georgia three.

When vacancies happen in the Representation from any State, the Executive Authority thereof shall issue Writs of Election to fill such Vacancies.

The House of Representatives shall chuse their Speaker and other Officers; and shall have the sole Power of Impeachment.

Section. 3. The Senate of the United States shall be composed of two Senators from each State, chosen by the Legislature thereof, for six Years; and each Senator shall have one Vote.

Immediately after they shall be assembled in Consequence of the first Election, they shall be divided as equally as may be into three Classes. The Seats of the Senators of the first Class shall be vacated at the Expiration of the second Year, of the second Class at the Expiration of the fourth Year, and of the third Class at the Expiration of the sixth Year, so that one third may be chosen every second Year; and if Vacancies happen by Resignation, or otherwise, during the Recess of the Legislature of any State, the Executive thereof may make temporary Appointments until the next Meeting of the Legislature, which shall then fill such Vacancies.

No Person shall be a Senator who shall not have attained to the Age of thirty Years, and been nine Years a Citizen of the United States, and who shall not, when elected, be an Inhabitant of that State for which he shall be chosen.

The Vice President of the United States shall be President of the Senate, but shall have no Vote, unless they be equally divided.

The Senate shall chuse their other Officers, and also a President pro tempore, in the Absence of the Vice President, or when he shall exercise the Office of President of the United States.

The Senate shall have the sole Power to try all Impeachments. When sitting for that Purpose, they shall be on Oath or Affirmation. When the President of the United States is tried, the Chief Justice shall preside: And no Person shall be convicted without the Concurrence of two thirds of the Members present.

Judgment in Cases of Impeachment shall not extend further than to removal from Office, and disqualification to hold and enjoy any Office of honor, Trust or Profit under the United States: but the Party convicted shall nevertheless be liable and subject to Indictment, Trial, Judgment and Punishment, according to Law.

Section. 4. The Times, Places and Manner of holding Elections for Senators and Representatives, shall be prescribed in each State by the Legislature thereof; but the Congress may at any time by Law make or alter such Regulations, except as to the Places of chusing Senators.

The Congress shall assemble at least once in every Year, and such Meeting shall be on the first Monday in December, unless they shall by Law appoint a different Day.

Section. 5. Each House shall be the Judge of the Elections, Returns and Qualifications of its own Members, and a Majority of each shall constitute a Quorum to do Business; but a smaller Number may adjourn from day to day, and may be authorized to compel the Attendance of absent Members, in such Manner, and under such Penalties as each House may provide.

Each House may determine the Rules of its Proceedings, punish its Members for disorderly Behaviour, and, with the Concurrence of two thirds, expel a Member.

Each House shall keep a Journal of its Proceedings, and from time to time publish the same, excepting such Parts as may in their Judgment require Secrecy; and the Yeas and Nays of the Members of either House on any question shall, at the Desire of one fifth of those Present, be entered on the Journal.

Neither House, during the Session of Congress, shall, without the Consent of the other, adjourn for more than three days, nor to any other Place than that in which the two Houses shall be sitting.

Section. 6. The Senators and Representatives shall receive a Compensation for their Services, to be ascertained by Law, and paid out of the Treasury of the United States. They shall in all Cases, except Treason, Felony and Breach of the Peace, be privileged from Arrest during their Attendance at the Session of their respective Houses, and in going to and returning from the same; and for any Speech or Debate in either House, they shall not be questioned in any other Place.

No Senator or Representative shall, during the Time for which he was elected, be appointed to any civil Office under the Authority of the United States, which shall have been created, or the Emoluments whereof shall have been encreased during such time; and no Person holding any Office under the United States, shall be a Member of either House during his Continuance in Office.

Section. 7. All Bills for raising Revenue shall originate in the House of Representatives; but the Senate may propose or concur with Amendments as on other Bills.

Every Bill which shall have passed the House of Representatives and the Senate, shall, before it become a Law, be presented to the President of the

CONSTITUTION OF THE UNITED STATES

Framed by James Madison and signed into law in 1787

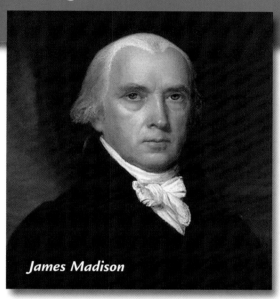

James Madison

WHAT WAS IT?

The Constitution was a document that explained in great detail how to run the new United States of America.

A FAMOUS PART

"We the People of the United States, in Order to form a more perfect Union, establish Justice, insure domestic Tranquility, provide for the common defense, promote the general Welfare, and secure the Blessings of Liberty to ourselves and our Posterity, do ordain and establish this Constitution for the United States of America."

WHAT MADISON SAID

America should have a government made up of three parts. One part will make the laws, one part will make sure the laws are carried out, and one part will review all the laws to make sure they do not go against the Constitution.

All three parts will have ways to make sure the other parts do not get too much power.

WHAT HAPPENED?

Our Constitution has stood the test of time and change. Many other nations have based their constitutions on ours. Madison also figured out a way to amend (change) parts of the Constitution that were not working with new amendments. The first ten amendments are called the Bill of Rights.

Signing the Constitution into law

By the President of the United States of America:

A Proclamation.

Whereas, on the twenty-second day of September, in the year of our Lord one thousand eight hundred and sixty-two, a proclamation was issued by the President of the United States, containing, among other things, the following, to wit:

"That on the first day of January, in the "year of our Lord one thousand eight hundred "and sixty-three, all persons held as slaves within "any State or designated part of a State, the people "whereof shall then be in rebellion against the "United States, shall be then, thenceforward, and "forever free; and the Executive Government of the "United States, including the military and naval "authority thereof, will recognize and maintain "the freedom of such persons, and will do no act "or acts to repress such persons, or any of them, "in any efforts they may make for their actual "freedom.

"That the Executive will, on the first day

THE EMANCIPATION PROCLAMATION

Written by Abraham Lincoln
January 1, 1863

WHAT WAS IT?

This document gave freedom to all enslaved people living in states that had broken away from the United States.

A FAMOUS PART

"I do order and declare that all persons held as slaves within said designated States, and parts of States, are, and henceforward shall be free;"

WHAT LINCOLN SAID

1. People who are being held as slaves in the states that have broken away from the Union are now free.
2. The United States will protect the rights of the freed slaves if anyone tries to harm them or recapture them.
3. Any freed slave who is willing and able to fight is welcome to join the Union Army.

WHAT HAPPENED?

It took awhile for word to spread about Lincoln's Emancipation Proclamation. As word reached slaves in the South, they put down their work tools and many marched North to join the Union Army.

Families packed up their things and moved to free states, and many went out west to build new towns.

FREE!

" MAKE WAY FOR LIBERTY.!"

Jackie Robinson came to march and hear Dr. King speak.

"I HAVE A DREAM" SPEECH

Dr. Martin Luther King. Jr, on the steps of the Lincoln Monument in Washington D.C. August 28, 1963

WHAT HAPPENED?

Over 200,000 people came to the Lincoln Memorial to demand equal rights. Millions more heard Dr. King on the radio and TV or read his words in the newspaper. His speech made a huge impact.

It took more than 40 years but one of his dreams came true when an African American was elected the President of the United States.

WHAT WAS IT?

One of the most famous speeches ever given; it was heard by millions of people around the world.

A FAMOUS PART

"I have a dream that my four children will one day live in a nation where they will not be judged by the color of their skin but by the content of their character. "

WHAT DR. KING SAID

1. It has been 100 years since Lincoln's Emancipation Proclamation, but even though slavery had ended, things are still very bad for African Americans.
2. Many African Americans are getting tired of being treated badly. Some have turned to violence because they are so angry. We have to keep trying to change things peacefully.
3. Somehow change will come if we just keep trying.
4. "I have a dream" that things will change and that black and white people will one day be friends and equals.
5. It will be so wonderful when that day finally comes—a day when everyone, from the Atlantic to the Pacific, is "Free at last!"

MAP OF VIRGINIA'S COUNTIES AND CITIES

Can you find your county or city on this map of our state?

Counties

Independent Cities

WEST VIRGINIA

KENTUCKY

TENNESSEE

Highland

Bath

Alleghany
Covington

Botetourt

Craig

Bedford
Bedford

Buchanan

Giles

Dickenson

Salem • • Roanoke

Montgomery
Roanoke

Wise

Bland

Pulaski • Radford

Tazewell

Norton

Russell

Wythe

Franklin

Lee

Smyth

Floyd

Scott

Washington

Carroll

Patrick

Bristol •

Grayson

Galax

Martinsville

Henry

Visiting Virginia from West to East

Wise County is coal country.

Bristol is on the border with Tennessee.

Roanoke is a fast-growing city.

Monticello, Jefferson's home, is in Charlottesville.

MARYLAND

WASHINGTON, D.C.

DELAWARE

NORTH CAROLINA

Frederick
Winchester
Clarke
Loudoun
Warren
Fairfax
Falls Church
Fairfax
Arlington
Shenandoah
Fauquier
Manassas
Manassas Park
Alexandria
Rappahannock
Prince William
Page
Rockingham
Culpeper
Stafford
Harrisonburg
Madison
Augusta
Greene
Orange
Fredericksburg
King George
Staunton
Spotsylvania
Westmoreland
Waynesboro
Charlottesville
Louisa
Caroline
Richmond
Northumberland
Rock-ridge
Albemarle
Fluvanna
Essex
Nelson
Hanover
King William
King & Queen
Lancaster
Lexington
Buena Vista
Goochland
Middlesex
Accomack
Amherst
Buckingham
Henrico
Powhatan
Richmond
New Kent
Matthews
Northampton
Lynchburg
Cumber-land
Chesterfield
Charles City
James City
Gloucester
York
Appomattox
Amelia
Hopewell
Williamsburg
Campbell
Prince Edward
Colonial Heights
Petersburg
Prince George
Newport News
Poquoson
Hampton
Nottoway
Dinwiddie
Surry
Charlotte
Lunenburg
Sussex
Isle of Wight
Norfolk
Portsmouth
Virginia Beach
Halifax
Brunswick
Suffolk
Chesapeake
Danville
Mecklenburg
Emporia
Greensville
Franklin
Southampton

N NE E SE S SW W NW

How Many of These Places Have You Seen?

Richmond is our state capital.

Williamsburg brings the 1700s to life.

Arlington is close to Washington, D.C.

The Eastern Shore has water on three sides.

UNITED STATES POLITICAL MAP

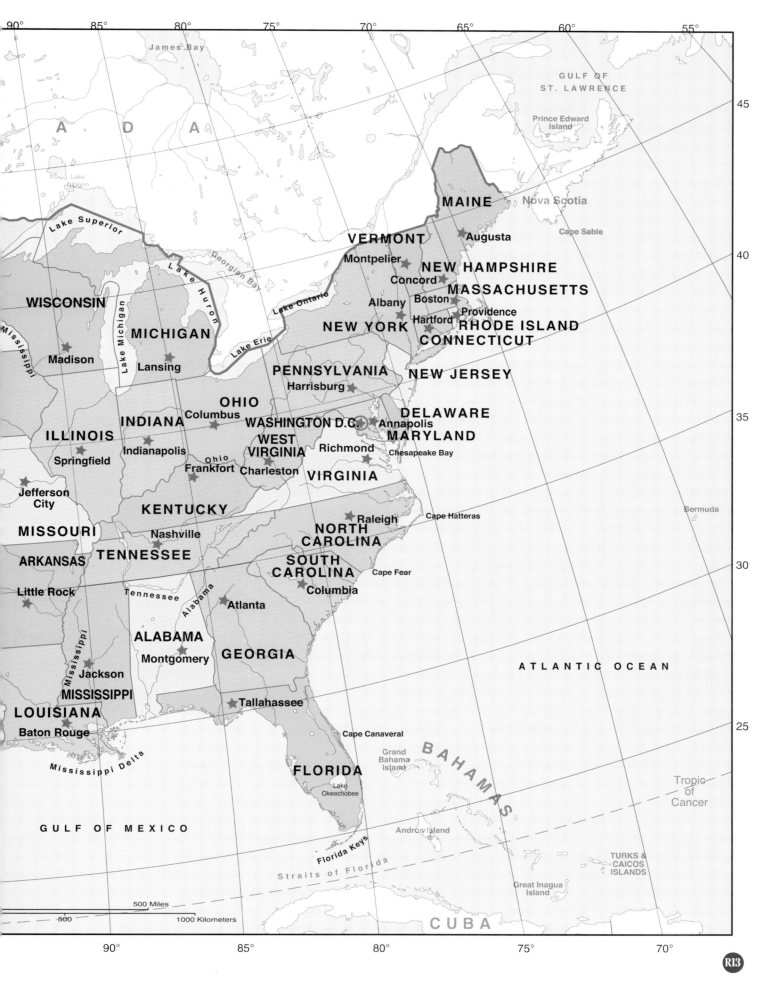

90°   85°   80°   75°   70°   65°   60°   55°

James Bay

GULF OF
ST. LAWRENCE   45

C   A   N   A   D   A
Prince Edward
Island

Lake
Nipigon
Lake Superior

Nova Scotia
MAINE
Cape Sable

Georgian Bay
Lake Huron   VERMONT   Augusta   40

Montpelier   NEW HAMPSHIRE
WISCONSIN   Lake Ontario   Concord   MASSACHUSETTS

Lake Michigan   MICHIGAN   Albany   Boston
Lake Erie   NEW YORK   Hartford Providence
Madison   Lansing   RHODE ISLAND
CONNECTICUT

PENNSYLVANIA   NEW JERSEY

OHIO   Harrisburg   35
INDIANA   Columbus   DELAWARE
ILLINOIS   WASHINGTON D.C. Annapolis
WEST   MARYLAND
Springfield   Indianapolis   VIRGINIA   Richmond   Chesapeake Bay
Ohio   Frankfort Charleston   VIRGINIA
Jefferson   Bermuda
City
KENTUCKY   Cape Hatteras
MISSOURI   Nashville   Raleigh
NORTH
ARKANSAS   TENNESSEE   CAROLINA   30

SOUTH
Little Rock   CAROLINA   Cape Fear
Tennessee   Alabama   Atlanta   Columbia
ALABAMA   ATLANTIC OCEAN
Jackson   Montgomery   GEORGIA
MISSISSIPPI
LOUISIANA   Tallahassee
Baton Rouge   25

Cape Canaveral
Mississippi Delta   Grand
Bahama   B A H A M A S   Tropic
Island   of
FLORIDA   Cancer
Lake
Okeechobee
GULF   OF   MEXICO
Andros Island
TURKS &
Florida Keys   CAICOS
ISLANDS
Straits of Florida   Great Inagua
Island

500 Miles

500
1000 Kilometers

C U B A

R13

90°   85°   80°   75°   70°

ARCTIC OCEAN

ASIA

CHUKCHI SEA

BERING SEA

St. Lawrence Island

BEAUFORT SEA

Pt. Barrow

GREENLAND

ICELAND

Ellesmere Island

Baffin Bay

Victoria Island

Baffin Island

Cape Dyer

Kap Farvel

Aleutian Islands

Kodiak Island

ALASKA (USA)
Mt. McKinley

Yukon

Porcupine

Mackenzie

Great Bear Lake

Mt. Logan
YUKON TERRITORY

GULF OF ALASKA

BRITISH COLUMBIA

MCKENZIE MOUNTAINS

NORTHWEST TERRITORIES

Great Slave Lake

N U N A V U T

LABRADOR SEA

Cape Chidley

Hudson Bay

QUEBEC

Labrador

NEWFOUNDLAND AND LABRADOR

Cape Bauld

Newfoundland

QUEEN CHARLOTTE ISLANDS

Peace

Athabasca

ALBERTA

N. Saskatchewan

S. Saskatchewan

SASKATCHEWAN

MANITOBA

CANADA

ONTARIO

Belcher Is.

PRINCE EDWARD IS.

NEW BRUNSWICK

NOVA SCOTIA

Mt. Kaatahdin

MAINE

Cape Sable

Cape Flattery

Mt. Rainier

WASHINGTON

Columbia

Missouri

NORTH DAKOTA

MONTANA

L. Superior

GREAT LAKES

L. Huron

VERMONT
NEW HAMPSHIRE
Mt. Washington

ADIRONDACK MTS.

Cape Cod

MASSACHUSETTS
RHODE ISLAND
CONNECTICUT

ROCKY MOUNTAINS

OREGON

IDAHO

COLUMBIA PLATEAU

WYOMING

BLACK HILLS

SOUTH DAKOTA

MINNESOTA

WISCONSIN

MICHIGAN

Michigan

NEW YORK

PENNSYLVANIA

NEW JERSEY

Cape Mendocino

GREAT BASIN

SIERRA NEVADA

Great Salt Lake

NEVADA

UTAH

Mt. Whitney

GREAT PLAINS

Platte

NEBRASKA

IOWA

Mississippi

ILLINOIS

INDIANA

OHIO

WEST VIRGINIA

DELAWARE
WASHINGTON D.C.
MARYLAND

VIRGINIA

APPALACHIAN MOUNTAINS

Cape Hatteras

BERMUDA

DEATH VALLEY

COLORADO PLATEAU

Colorado

COLORADO

Arkansas

KANSAS

MISSOURI

KENTUCKY

TENNESSEE

NORTH CAROLINA

COASTAL PLAIN

Pt. Arguello

CALIFORNIA

MOJAVE DESERT

ARIZONA

SONORA DESERT

NEW MEXICO

Canadian

INTERIOR PLAINS

OZARK PLATEAU

UNITED STATES OF AMERICA

OKLAHOMA

ARKANSAS

Red

Mississippi

Alabama

SOUTH CAROLINA

GEORGIA

ATLANTIC OCEAN

Punta Eugenia

GULF OF CALIFORNIA

Baja California

TEXAS

Colorado

Rio Grande

LOUISIANA

MISSISSIPPI

ALABAMA

GULF COASTAL PLAIN

Mississippi Delta

FLORIDA

Cape Fear

Cabo Falso

MEXICO

GULF OF MEXICO

BAHAMAS

CUBA

DOMINICAN REPUBLIC

PACIFIC OCEAN

0   1000 Miles

0   500   1000   1500 Kilometers

Cabo Corrientes

Yucatan Peninsula

HAITI

JAMAICA

PUERTO RICO

CARIBBEAN SEA

BELIZE

GUATEMALA

HONDURAS

EL SALVADOR

NICARAGUA

COSTA RICA

PANAMA

SOUTH AMERICA

160°   HAWAII   155°

Kauai
Mt. Kawaikini

Nihau

Kauai Channel

Oahu

Honolulu   Molokai

Lanai   Kahoolawe   Maui

Kahoolawe

Mauna Kea
Hilo
Hawaii
Mauna Loa   Kilauea Crater

20°

PACIFIC OCEAN

0   50   100   150 Miles

0   50 100   200 Kilometers

NORTH AMERICA and HAWAII PHYSICAL MAP

R14

NORTH AMERICA and HAWAII POLITICAL MAP

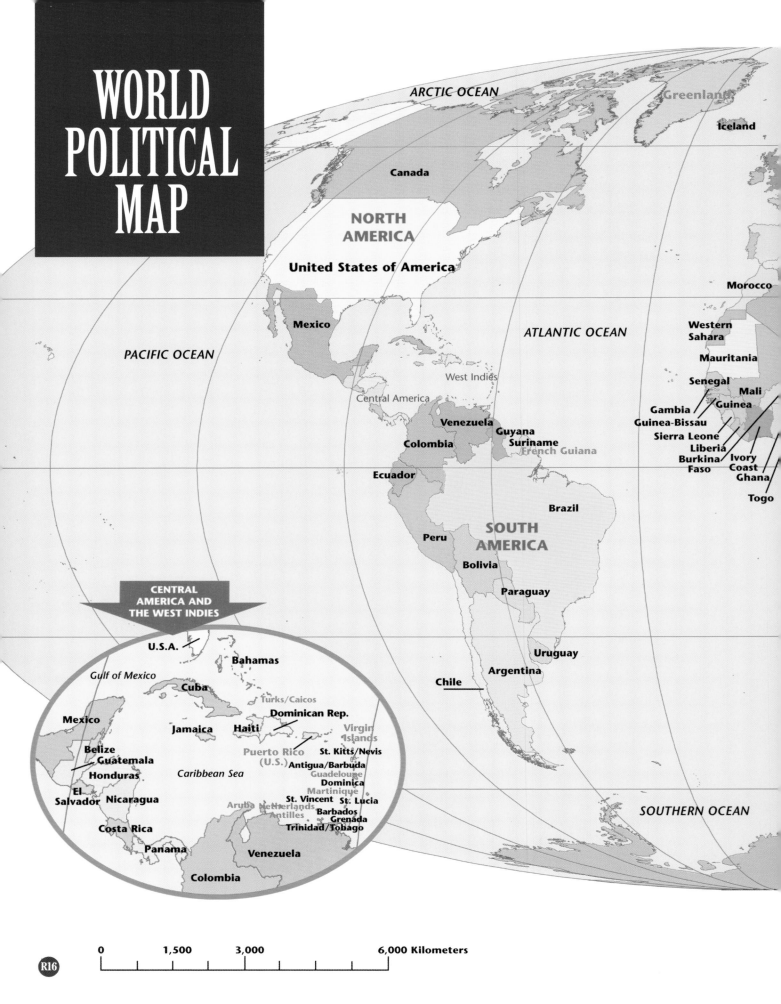

WORLD POLITICAL MAP

ARCTIC OCEAN

Greenland

Iceland

Canada

NORTH AMERICA

United States of America

Morocco

Mexico

ATLANTIC OCEAN

Western Sahara

Mauritania

PACIFIC OCEAN

West Indies

Senegal

Mali

Central America

Gambia

Guinea

Venezuela

Guyana

Guinea-Bissau

Colombia

Suriname

Sierra Leone

French Guiana

Liberia

Ivory Coast

Ecuador

Burkina Faso

Ghana

Togo

Brazil

Peru

SOUTH AMERICA

Bolivia

Paraguay

CENTRAL AMERICA AND THE WEST INDIES

Uruguay

U.S.A.

Bahamas

Argentina

Gulf of Mexico

Chile

Cuba

Turks/Caicos

Mexico

Dominican Rep.

Jamaica

Haiti

Virgin Islands

Belize

Puerto Rico (U.S.)

St. Kitts/Nevis

Guatemala

Antigua/Barbuda

Honduras

Caribbean Sea

Guadeloupe

Dominica

El Salvador

Nicaragua

Martinique

St. Vincent

St. Lucia

Aruba Netherlands Antilles

Barbados

Costa Rica

Grenada

Trinidad/Tobago

Panama

Venezuela

Colombia

SOUTHERN OCEAN

0   1,500   3,000   6,000 Kilometers

R16

ARCTIC OCEAN

ASIA

EUROPE

Russia

Kazakhstan

Mongolia

Georgia
Armenia
Turkey
Azerbaijan
Uzbekistan
Kyrgyzstan
Turkmenistan
Tajikistan

N. Korea
S. Korea
Japan
China

Cyprus
Lebanon
Israel
Syria
Iraq
Iran
Afghanistan

Tunisia

Algeria
Libya
Egypt
Jordan
Saudi
Arabia
Kuwait
Bahrain
Qatar
United
Arab
Emirates
Oman
Pakistan
Nepal
Bhutan
India
Myanmar
Laos
Taiwan

PACIFIC OCEAN

AFRICA

Niger
Chad
Sudan
Eritrea
Yemen
Djibouti
Bangladesh
Thailand
Vietnam
Cambodia
Philippines

Nigeria
Central
African Rep.
Cameroon
Ethiopia
Somalia
Uganda
Kenya
Sri Lanka
Brunei
Malaysia
Singapore

Benin
Gabon
Equatorial
Guinea
Dem.
Rep. Congo
Rwanda
Burundi
Tanzania
Rep.
Congo

Guam
(U.S.)

Papua
New Guinea
Solomon
Islands

INDIAN OCEAN

Indonesia

Angola
Zambia
Mozambique
Malawi
Madagascar
Zimbabwe
Botswana
Namibia

Fiji

COUNTRIES IN
EUROPE

AUSTRALIA
Australia

Swaziland
South
Africa
Lesotho

New Zealand

Sweden
Finland
Norway
Estonia
Latvia
Lithuania
Russia

United
Kingdom
Denmark
Belarus
Ireland
Netherlands
Germany
Poland
Belgium
Liechtenstein
Czech Rep.
Slovakia
Ukraine
Luxembourg
France
Switzerland
Austria
Hungary
Moldova
Slovenia
Romania
Portugal
Monaco
Croatia
Serbia
Bosnia
Montenegro
Bulgaria
ANTARCTICA
Andorra
San
Marino
Italy
Vatican
City
Albania
Macedonia
Spain
Greece
Turkey
Mediterranean Sea

Black Sea

Malta
Algeria
Tunisia

0   1,500   3,000   6,000 Miles

GLOSSARY

Arch

(artch)

A curved stone construction that spans an opening and supports weight above it.

Architects

(ark-ih-tekts)

People who design buildings.

Architecture

(ark-ih-tek-chur)

The design of buildings.

Boycott

(BOY-cot)

To refuse to do business with a person, company, or nation in order to punish or show disapproval.

Capital Resources

(CAP-it-ul • RE sor-siz)

Goods made by people and used to produce other goods and services.

Caravan

(CARE-uh-van)

A long line of camels traveling together carrying people and goods.

Characteristics

(cahr-ick-tuh-RIS-tix)

Different traits that describe a person or place and its size, shape, or the way it looks.

Civil Disobediance

(SIV-ull • DIS-oh-BEE-dee-ens)

Refusing to obey laws that are unfair; using non-violent public protests, such as a group of people blocking the entrance to a building.

Civilization

(Siv-ill-a-zay-shun)

People in an advanced stage of development, with government, art, music, and public services such as running water, armies, or libraries.

Column

(col-um)

A tall cylinder-shaped pillar used to support a structure.

Communities

(com-YOU-nit-eez)

Places where people live, work, and play.

Contributions

(con-trib-YOU-shunz)

Acts of giving or doing something positive.

Customs

(CUST-umz)

Ways of doing things that are passed from one generation to the next.

Desegregation

(dee-seg-ra-GAY-shun)

The mixing of racial or religious groups together into a community after they have been kept apart.

Direct Democracy

(dy-REKT • duh-MOCK-ruh-see)

A government in which people vote to make their own rules and laws.

Diversity

(Di-VER-sit-ee)

The differences between people such as age, religion, and race.

Economic choice

(EK-uh-nom-ic • CHOYS)

The choice of, or decision among, alternatives or possibilities.

Equality

(ee-KWALL-a-tee)

Treating all people exactly the same way.

Equator

(ee-KWAY-tur)

An imaginary line around the middle of the Earth that divides the globe into the Northern and Southern Hemispheres.

Ethnic origin

(ETH-nick • OR-uh-jin)

People who share a common race, birthplace, religion, language, or culture.

European

(Your-a-PEA-in)

A person from one of the countries in Europe.

Explorer

(ex-PLORE-ur

A person who travels seeking new discoveries.

Federal

(FED-er-ul)

Relating to a system in which power is shared between the central government and a group of states.

Goods

Things that people make or use to satisfy needs and wants.

Government

(GUV-urn-mint

A group of people who makes rules and laws, carries out rules and laws, and decides if rules and laws have been broken.

Hemisphere

(HEM-iss-fear)

Half of a sphere (globe) created by the Prime Meridian or the Equator.

Human Resources

(HUE-min • RE-sors-is)

People working to produce goods and services.

Laws

Important rules written and carried out by the government.

Migrant

(MY-grint)

A person who moves from place to place seeking work.

Natural Resources

(NATCH-ur-ul • RE sor-siz)

Useful materials that come from nature.

Opportunity cost

(opp-ur-TOO-nit-ee • COST)

The next best choice that is given up when a decision is made.

Prime Meridian

(PRIME • mur-ID-ee-an)

An imaginary line that (when extended completely around the Earth) divides the globe into the Eastern and Western Hemispheres.

Producers

(Pro-DOO-sirs)

People who use resources to make goods and/or provide services.

Region

(REE-jon)

Places that have common characteristics.

Representative Democracy

(rep-ree-SENT-a-tive duh-MOCK-ruh-see)

A government in which people vote for (elect) a smaller group of citizens to represent them and to make rules and laws for everyone.

Republic

(ree-PUB-lick)

A government in which the power is given to its citizens who choose people to represent them.

Republican form of government

A representative democracy where we elect people to speak for us in the making of laws.

Rights

(RITES)

Freedoms that we are all entitled to from birth. Life, liberty, and the pursuit of happiness are examples of rights.

Rules

What people must or must not do.

Segregation

(seg-re-GAY-shun)

The act or practice of keeping people or groups apart, which leads to inequality.

Services

(SIR-vis-is)

Activities that satisfy people's needs and wants.

Specialization

(Spesh-uh-li-ZAY-shun)

What occurs when people focus on the production of selected goods and services.

Union

(YOU-nyun)

A group of people who work to improve conditions and wages at a company.

Veteran

(VET-ur-in)

A person who has served in the military, which includes the Army, Navy, Air Force, Marines, Coast Guard, and National Guard.

INDEX